'A thought-provoking insight into leadership, drawing on the world of sport to identify key drivers for business leaders.'

Baroness Sue Campbell, Director of Women's Football, FA

'As a business leader I recognize we can learn a lot from sport. *Staying the Distance* sets out 13 lessons in a clear and powerful way.'

Richard Harpin, Founder and CEO, HomeServe Plc and Growth Partner

'Catherine's book demonstrates the important lessons that sports can teach us about life. It's a must-read.'

Debbie Wosskow OBE, Co-Founder and NED, AllBright

'Catherine successfully weaves together her own extensive experiences and those of some of the great leadership experts out there into a very engaging book. It is a great read with real takeaways for aspiring and experienced leaders alike.'

Stuart Lancaster OBE, Senior Coach, Leinster Rugby

'Fascinating and insightful. Drawing on her incredible depth and breadth of knowledge about sport and leadership, Catherine Baker reveals the deeper leadership lessons that lie within sport if we look beneath the shiny surface. Ensuring we see beyond superficial motivational clichés, this book offers leaders an in-depth tour of some vital and overlooked leadership insights from sport.'

Cath Bishop, Olympic rowing medallist, former diplomat, leadership & culture coach, author of *The Long Win*

'We may see our sporting icons as superhuman, but their achievements have lessons for us all. In this wise and invigorating book, Catherine Baker breaks down the secrets of sustainable success in any domain, with timeless insights into the habits of high-flyers. You will learn how to meet your own goals and to encourage optimum performance in others. It is essential reading for any leader.'

David Robson, Author of *The Expectation Effect*

'There are so many invaluable lessons to be learned from the world of elite sports – *Staying the Distance* takes many of the best ones and shows exactly how they can, and deserve to be, incorporated into business life.'

Col Dame Kelly Holmes (MBE Mil)

'Catherine has delivered a seriously inspiring book of learnings and anecdotes that doesn't preach. Real stories of real leaders that we all know, [mostly] love and how to learn from their successes and mistakes. Definitely one for a regular dip into... if you'd don't make it all the way through in one sitting.'

Annamarie Phelps CBE OLY

'By adjusting our mindset we can turn threats into challenges and anxiety into excitement, and by doing so perform at our best. This book introduces us to the psychological trials and tribulations of some of our greatest sporting icons and links them to day-to-day leadership challenges. Suddenly it's possible to relate in a new way to legends like Serena Williams or Chris Hoy.'

Stephanie Hilborne OBE, Chief Executive, Women in Sport

'Whether it is lessons, prompts, insights or a really pithy quotation – if you are looking for support in navigating the difficult challenges of leadership, Catherine has written an excellent book to support your journey. Drawing from her own experiences of how sport can help guide you through life, *Staying the Distance* is definitely recommended reading.'

Tim Hollingsworth OBE, Chief Executive, Sport England

'This book is a must read for all leaders. It has opened my eyes and challenged my thinking. I love the way the book is structured. Each lesson is grounded in academic research but provides case studies, shares stories and offers practical tips that can be applicable to all. Attaining long-term success is a goal all leaders should strive to achieve and this book is a perfect guide in how you can accomplish that.'

Maggie Alphonsi MBE, England Rugby World Cup winner and Broadcaster

'At first glance, the worlds of sport and business may feel very different, but as this book amply demonstrates, there's much for the ambitious business leader to learn from the experiences of our most successful sports people.'

Kate Waters, Director of Client Strategy and Planning, ITV

'Catherine Baker knows exactly what makes elite sports people so successful: a combination of resilience and stamina that, when combined with the most effective training programmes, can lead to sustainable performance in the long term. *Staying the Distance* frames those concepts for a business audience and offers readers a unique perspective on exactly how to perfect their leadership skillset.'

Judy Murray OBE

'In this guide to purposeful and values-based leadership, Catherine draws on the world of sport to illustrate her key lessons - how to engage, challenge and support both yourself and your teams to deliver consistent high performance, and, importantly, how to sustain this. It's a marathon rather than a sprint!'

Jenny Harrison, CFO at enfinium and founder player at Harlequin Ladies RFC

'As the role of leadership evolves, *Staying the Distance* is essential reading for anyone looking to improve their leadership credentials. Catherine Baker's authenticity and personable style shine throughout this outstanding book as she brings her passion for the subject to life, sharing experiences and giving her unique perspective on the relationship between elite sports and business leadership.'

Dan Kayne, Founder, O Shaped

'Catherine Baker's *Staying the Distance* is a wonderful dose of writing that makes the reader reflect on their career journey through relevant anecdotes we can all relate to, with reference to athletes we know and love! I couldn't put it down. The concepts in Catherine's book make us take a long deep look at our lives and how we can influence our own success on many levels. *Staying the Distance* is one of those books that makes you feel like anything is possible....we are capable of so much more than we think we are!'

Audrey Klein, Board Member, Planet Smart City, SFO and Great Ormond Street Hospital

'I've never seen a leadership textbook – until now. This is the best read for anyone in leadership who means to make a difference, both in what they do and how they do it. Catherine Baker has joined the list of top influencers in my career, and I will pick this book up regularly as an essential aide memoire – you'll read it more than once! Utterly brilliant.'

Tara Dillon, CEO, CIMSPA

With a foreword by Gareth Southgate

STAYING

THE

DISTANCE

The lessons from sport that
business leaders have been missing

CATHERINE BAKER

BLOOMSBURY BUSINESS
LONDON · OXFORD · NEW YORK · NEW DELHI · SYDNEY

BLOOMSBURY BUSINESS
Bloomsbury Publishing Plc
50 Bedford Square, London, WC1B 3DP, UK
29 Earlsfort Terrace, Dublin 2, Ireland

BLOOMSBURY, BLOOMSBURY BUSINESS and the Diana logo are trademarks
of Bloomsbury Publishing Plc

First published in Great Britain 2023

A catalogue record for this book is available from the British Library

Library of Congress Cataloguing-in-Publication data has been applied for

ISBN: 978-1-3994-0585-0; eBook: 978-1-3994-0586-7

2 4 6 8 10 9 7 5 3 1

Typeset by Deanta Global Publishing Services, Chennai, India
Printed and bound in Great Britain by CPI Group (UK) Ltd, Croydon CR0 4YY

To find out more about our authors and books visit www.bloomsbury.com
and sign up for our newsletters

To my mother Judy Whiteman who, throughout all that life has thrown at her, has quietly and consistently demonstrated immense strength, stoicism and stamina

Contents

PART TWO

Getting the Best Out of Those You Lead   **101**

Foreword by Gareth Southgate

It was always my belief that there was far more alignment between business and sport than people might have imagined. Of course the technical detail is different. Results are not judged quarterly, but sometimes three or four times a week and the dynamic of your 'shareholders' sitting in the stadium with a very vocal opinion is slightly different to the normal AGM. In either environment, management and, perhaps more pertinently, leadership has never been more challenging, more closely scrutinized and more vulnerable to rapid change. The VUCA world!

By sharing stories, experiences and concepts within this book, Catherine has provided an opportunity for any leader to reflect, learn and upskill. From managing yourself, to better understanding the motivations of your athletes or business colleagues, I found innumerable examples of situations or emotions I had lived through. Everyone will have a unique take, because we are all at different stages of our learning, with our own experiences and consequently all see the world slightly differently. Nevertheless, I believe every manager/leader will find either new ideas or valuable reminders of what they 'should be doing' within this book.

Best wishes,
GS
England Men's Football Manager
March 2023

Introduction

'I always describe sport as the university of life... Because you have everything: extreme challenge; success; defeat; times when you make super progress; and other times when things go stale.'

Mel Marshall, coach to multiple Olympic Gold Medallist
and World Record Holder, Adam Peaty

We are very used to drawing lessons from sport and applying them to business. Much of these focus on high performance; on winning or on achieving your goals. But we've all been missing a trick. Day in, day out, sport has been showing us not just how to improve, perform and achieve, but how to do so on a sustainable basis. How to get the best out of yourself, and those you lead, consistently, over the long term.

Now, more than ever, these lessons are needed. Too many senior leaders have neared or reached burnout over the last few years. Too many of those they lead have also struggled, trying to maintain and improve their performance amid challenging circumstances of the like not seen for many years. It's not just about high performance in the moment, but how we can perform over the long term – in other words, how we can stay the distance.

For a long time I have been fascinated by the research and insight that comes out of the world of sport and relates to human potential and performance. One paper that particularly caught my eye was the Great British Medallists Research Study: A Summary[1]. This paper, written and distributed within performance sport during the Rio

---

[1] S. Laing, L. Hardy, C. Warr, The Great British Medallists Research Study: A Summary.

Olympic Games cycle, summarized key findings from a research project carried out between 2010 and 2014 involving a collaboration between UK Sport, Bangor University, Exeter University and Cardiff Metropolitan University[2]. The project's aim was to comprehensively compare and identify differences and commonalities in the developmental biographies of high-achieving British athletes. Three main factors were identified as important contributors to success in both groupings of athletes examined (elite and super-elite):

- These athletes were brought up in families where they were exposed to a 'culture of striving'. This was demonstrated in one or more of the following ways:
  - there was an environment and expectation of achievement;
  - there was a strong work ethic;
  - the environment was highly competitive; or
  - high value was placed on mastery ('being the best that you can be') and outcome ('achieving goals');
- They demonstrated a very high level of conscientiousness towards sport;
- They demonstrated a very high level of commitment to training.

---

[2] Rees, T., Hardy, L., Abernethy, B., Güllich, A., Côté, J., Woodman, T., Montgomery, H., Laing, S., & Warr, C. (2015). *What Underpins the Performance of Serial Gold-Medal Winners? A Review of Current Knowledge into the Development of the World's Best Talent*, in preparation.

Hardy, L., Laing, S., Barlow, M., Kuncheva, L., Evans, L., Rees, T., Woodman, T., Abernethy, B., Güllich, A., Côté, J., Warr, C., Jackson, A., Wraith, L., & Kavanagh, J. (2013). *Great British Medallists: A Comparison of the Biographies of GB Super-Elite and Elite Athletes*. End of project report submitted to UK Sport (345 pages).

Barlow, M., Hardy, L., Evans, L., Rees, T., & Woodman, T. (2015). *Great British Medallists: A Comparison of the Psychosocial Biographies of GB Super-Elite and Elite Athletes*, in preparation.

What has always stayed with me on reading this report is this focus on striving, on consciously wanting to continue to improve, while understanding the commitment it takes to ensure this. However, one of the challenges around such striving – this drive to continuously improve – is how to do so in a way that ensures performance can be sustained. It is this that makes it possible to stay the distance.

This focus on aiming for the best can, if not managed in the right way, have adverse consequences. And as in sport, so in leadership. Leadership can be hard. It can be daunting. And it can be relentless. This is the case at the best of times and even more so in periods of extreme pressure and uncertainty, such as we have all recently gone through with the COVID-19 pandemic.

Sport has always been central to my life. Through playing. Through coaching. Through volunteering. Through supporting. Through continuing my habit of turning to the sports pages first of any newspaper I read. But also with my professional hat on: both through building and sharing expertise around what makes a good coach and through working with and beside (and gaining significant insight into) elite athletes.

Alongside sport, leadership is another deep interest, one where I read whatever I can get my hands on, study and in which I have gained in-depth insight, not least through coaching senior leaders across different business sectors. And over time I have come to an important realization; one that is especially relevant at this time, with everything that senior leaders have been facing. Sport has been showing us all along how to improve, perform and achieve over the long term. The lessons have been hidden in plain sight, we've just been shining the spotlight in the wrong place. It's as if we've been focusing on the lessons around how to build strength and speed, but all this time we've been ignoring the lessons on how to build the stamina needed to consistently perform well over a sustained period of time.

In this book we will uncover these lessons: the ones that have been hiding in plain sight. We will hear stories from a variety of elite athletes and coaches. We will anchor them with cutting-edge research and business case studies and provide guidance for each lesson on how to deploy them in your leadership.

Each lesson is brought to life with a case study at the end of the chapter: the characters and stories are wholly imaginary although based on examples and situations that I have come across over the years.

Part One focuses on the six lessons that will enable you to get the best out of yourself over the long term. In Part Two we turn to the seven lessons that will enable you to get the best out of those you lead on a sustained basis. In choosing these lessons, I have remained focused on two elements: the topic must be fundamental to long-term performance and it must be one on which sport has some incredibly relevant, but usually hidden, insight to share. Each of these lessons form a vital part of the recipe for long-term success; while many leaders might understand and deploy a selection of them, I believe that in our current environment, all are vital. If you see consistent performance as something to strive for, to sustain for yourself and to encourage in others over the long term, then this book is your roadmap.

PART ONE

Getting the Best Out of *You*

'*Your attitude, not your aptitude, will determine your altitude.*'

Hilary Hinton 'Zig' Ziglar, American author and speaker

How you approach your job as a leader, and how you show up for work every day, is key to how you perform. The attitudes and approach you bring to your role, the behaviours that you demonstrate and the beliefs that you hold are fundamental to the impact you have. Not just in the short term but over the long term as well. How you approach your job as a leader is central to your ability to sustain your performance. To stay the distance.

This is an area that sport has been learning and demonstrating, day in day out. And it's an area that has been largely overlooked, with much of the focus being on high performance and winning. Taking this insight from sport, overlaying it with research and insight from the world of work more generally, a pattern clearly emerges around the attitudes and approach that can make all the difference. Connect this with the reality for many senior leaders on the ground and it becomes clear that these lessons from sport are game-changing, relevant and actionable.

In Part One we shine a spotlight on the key attitudes, approaches, behaviours and beliefs that drive long-term success for you as a leader and explore how you can apply them to your daily working life, with simple, practical and tangible steps.

CHAPTER ONE

How to Find Your Confidence Sweet Spot

'Practice creates confidence. Confidence empowers you.'

Simone Biles, American gymnast

Dame Kelly Holmes is a British middle-distance runner who famously won two Golds at the Athens Olympics in 2004. These Olympics were her last roll of the dice in a career that had been beset by injury and 'almosts'. Winning both the 800m and 1500m events was an amazing achievement and the highlight for the GB squad in that Olympic Games. This was the era when the team was still languishing in the medals table, with the impressive hauls of London 2012, Rio 2016 and Tokyo 2020 still a far-off dream.

What does Holmes feel was the springboard to success in her career? Racing against men. Not only did this drive her performance, but it instilled in Holmes a familiarity with pushing herself with and against people who were better than her. Alongside improving her times, she believes this gave her confidence – and we know that confidence is vital for success in elite sport.

Hot on the heels of her retirement, in 2008 Holmes set up a charity, the Dame Kelly Holmes Trust. In 2015, the Trust commissioned some research by Professor David Lavallee, the pre-eminent academic on athlete transition and duty of care. Lavallee was asked to look at athletes' ability to be high-performing *beyond* sport. The findings were positive and in particular confidence was highlighted as one of the key attributes of ex-elite athletes that enabled them to be successful across a diverse range of roles.[1]

What sits behind this confidence? Why do we so often hear athletes talking about crossing the white line (into their field of play), knowing they have done all they can to give of their best on that day? And what can we take into our own role as leaders?

Am I good enough? It's a fundamental question whether you are an elite athlete or in a position of leadership. And one which I know from experience sits in the head of many of the best athletes and many of the best leaders.

What's your answer?

Well, I can tell you that in most cases, the answer will be yes and no. You are probably good enough to some extent but you could always be better. And that's OK.

The right level of confidence is central to sustained performance – the confidence that gives you enough assurance to deliver and perform, balanced with an awareness that you are not the finished article and can always improve. This is the confidence sweet spot. This is the case whether you are an elite athlete or a leader.

How Do We Get This Wrong?

Confidence can have lots of different faces. We've all seen them. There's the bombast. The strutting. The putting on a mask. The inauthentic confidence. The confidence which crumbles when put under sustained pressure. Then there's the opposite end of the spectrum. Too little confidence. Too much of an imposter syndrome, where not only do you feel that you are not good enough, but also don't believe that you will ever be.

---

[1] https://www.damekellyholmestrust.org/more-than-medals-research

Too much confidence and you risk over-promising and under-delivering. Not helping those around you. Losing the trust of your team. And you will most likely stunt your own development (why work hard at getting better if you are brilliant already?). And as Artificial Intelligence (AI) transforms the nature of work, leaders who continue to believe they know it all are simply going to get caught out.

Too little confidence will similarly hamper your ability to improve, perform and achieve over the long term. If your lack of confidence prevents you from challenging yourself, prevents you from doing, prevents you from trying, you are not going to benefit from the growth that follows.

What we want to aim for is real, sustainable, long-term confidence. The sweet spot that marries belief that you can achieve, with an understanding of the need to, and process for, consistently getting better. So, what does sport teach us? What are the lessons that have been hiding in plain sight?

Sustaining Your Performance

It all starts with a bicycle.[2]

Are you able to ride a bicycle? If the answer is yes, were you born able to ride a bicycle? (This is not a trick question!) Cast your mind back to the process of learning how to ride your bike. What went into it? You probably wanted to learn in order to catch up with your friends, siblings or parents. You believed that you could learn, as you had seen others learn. You will have put in quite a bit of time and effort, and some of that will have involved pushing yourself out of your comfort zone, not least when the stabilizers were removed. You will no doubt have failed to some extent, with the failures probably

---

[2] With thanks to the team at https://thelearnerlab.com/, where I first came across this analogy.

involving a bit of pain (as you fell off the bike). And you will have received feedback on how you were doing, either directly ('I fell off, I need to do something differently next time') or via the person helping you to learn. You took that feedback on board as you focused your efforts on that magical moment when you would be confidently riding your bike into the distance. In essence, you will have demonstrated a growth mindset: the starting point to the confidence sweet spot.

The anchor

Some of you reading this will be familiar with the term 'growth mindset' and the significant amounts of research behind it. The phrase was first coined by an American academic called Carol Dweck as a result of lengthy research into mindsets and their impact on success. Making a distinction between a fixed mindset and a growth mindset, Dweck has shown that a belief that talents and abilities can be developed through effort, good teaching and persistence can help us fulfil our potential.

You might be wondering why a book that purports to be sharing hidden lessons from sport is starting with a concept that: (a) is well known; and (b) was born in the field of education. I know I would be. Well, sport has been living and breathing this concept, right under our noses. Dweck recognized this back in 2006 when she said: 'Athletes with the growth mindset find success in doing their best, in learning and improving.'[3]

What many leaders haven't done is truly understand how the concept breaks down and how to play it out in the workplace. And this is where sport can help us. A growth mindset is a belief in, a desire to and an approach for improvement. In other words, for getting better.

---

[3] Carol Dweck, *Mindset: The New Psychology of Success*, Random House, 2006.

And in sport, the concept is often broken down into four elements: effort, challenge, mistakes/failure and feedback.

Those with a growth mindset will put effort in, as they understand and believe that this can lead to improvement. They are happy to challenge themselves and push themselves out of their comfort zone as this is where real growth comes, with the added benefit of becoming increasingly comfortable with challenge. Just think back to Kelly Holmes' appreciation of the value of this at the start of the chapter. Holmes joins a long line of athletes, past and present, who have truly understood this. We began this book with a quote from Mel Marshall, coach to current world-beating swimmer, Adam Peaty. Peaty has aimed not just to win, but to transform his sport and leave a lasting legacy. He consistently pushes the boundaries of what is possible in his discipline (breaststroke) and does so by constantly challenging himself in his training regime, taking himself out of his comfort zone and trying new things in order to improve and perform over the long term.

Those with a growth mindset recognize that along with this willingness to challenge themselves comes the risk of failure or of making mistakes. And they are comfortable with that, on the basis that all of this is in pursuit of getting better over the long term. This makes them much less brittle when things don't go to plan and not only do they welcome feedback as a source of development and improvement, they actively seek it out. Someone with more of a fixed mindset struggles to see the link between effort and improvement and so, when taken to its logical end, why bother? Doing things beyond their current capabilities opens the door to something less than success, so why risk it? Mistakes and failure are to be avoided at all cost in case they look bad and feedback is unhelpful and unnecessary as ability is fixed in any event.

Look back to that quote from Carol Dweck and note what she is focusing on: the process, rather than the outcome – something we will pick up on again as we go through the book. And something that is central to the ability to build our growth mindset muscle.

So, sport has, for a long time, been demonstrating what growth mindset actually looks like in action. And if we don't believe that we can improve, develop and get better, and if we don't truly understand the process for doing so, we are not going to be able to get the best out of ourselves on a sustained basis; over the long term. We will reach a point, plateau and then fade. And who wants that? Don't you aspire for more? It is central to the confidence sweet spot and central to everything else that we cover here in this book.

Before we uncover more hidden lessons in this area, let's just acknowledge some of the links that have already been made in the business world with respect to growth mindset.

Back in the late 1990s, Jim Collins, the well-known business consultant, set out to discover what made some companies move from being good to being great. So, what enabled them to make that leap and stay there? Collins and his team embarked on a five-year study, selecting 11 companies whose stock returns had skyrocketed relative to other companies in their industry and who had maintained this edge for at least 15 years. They matched each company to another one in the same industry that had similar resources but did not make the leap. They also studied a third group of companies that had made the leap but could not sustain it. What distinguished the thriving companies from the others? Several important factors, as Collins reported in his book, *Good to Great*[4]. And as Dweck highlights in her own book, *Mindset: Changing the Way you Think to Fulfil Your Potential*,[5] there was one that was absolutely key in every case: the

---

[4] Jim Collins, *Good to Great: Why Some Companies Make the Leap…and Others Don't*, New York, Harper-Collins, 2001.

[5] Carol Dweck, *Mindset: Changing the Way you Think to Fulfil Your Potential*, Robinson, 2012, p. 110.

type of leader who led the company into greatness. Rather than being the larger-than-life, charismatic types full of ego and self-proclaimed talent, they were self-effacing people who constantly asked questions and had the ability to confront the most brutal answers; who could look failure in the face while maintaining faith that they would succeed in the end. Essentially, they had a growth mindset as opposed to a fixed mindset. They were not constantly trying to prove that they were better than others, but they were constantly trying to **improve**.

Conversely, looking at the famous failure of Enron (the American energy company whose accounting fraud led to its collapse with reverberations around the world) in 2001, many commentators put this down to a failure of mindset. Enron was talent-obsessed, creating a culture that worshipped talent, and so forcing employees to look and act extraordinarily talented. It basically forced them into a fixed mindset, the opposite of a growth mindset![6]

You might be questioning and reflecting on where you sit on the scale between a fixed and a growth mindset. And it's important to note that it is indeed a scale – it's not that each of us is one or the other. In fact, you will probably be able to recognize areas of your life where you are able to exhibit more of a growth mindset and those where it's more of a fixed mindset. Sport tells us that a focus on the process of improvement, combined with a desire to continually do so, and a belief that you can, will all help push us into the growth mindset zone. So, we have the central anchor: growth mindset. With some useful clarity from sport (which has been showing us all along) on how to apply it. Let's now turn to the other lessons from sport that have been hiding in plain sight, all geared towards finding the confidence sweet spot.

---

[6] Carol Dweck, *Mindset: Changing the Way you Think to Fulfil Your Potential*, Robinson, 2012, p. 110.

Play to Your Strengths

Think back to the breakdown of growth mindset: effort; challenge, mistakes/failure and feedback. What can we learn from sport about where best to deploy the first element – effort?

There is a natural tendency among our species to worry about what we're not good at. In my tennis game, my forehand is my main weapon. My backhand can be a bit suspect at times so what do I tend to spend most of my time worrying and thinking about … my backhand! It's often the same in the workplace. The tendency might therefore be when we think about deploying the effort encouraged by a growth mindset to focus on developing our areas of weakness, aiming to improve in those. The world of professional sport, however, presents us with a whole other way of looking at this: looking to, and leveraging, your natural strengths.

'Do not let what you cannot do interfere with what you can do.'

John Wooden, American basketball coach

Any good coach, presented with a new athlete to develop, will automatically look at where their strengths lie and see how they can develop those even further. Steffi Graf is one of the most successful tennis players of all time, winning 22 Grand Slam singles titles and holding the No. 1 world-ranking spot for a record 377 weeks. The incredible thing about Graf's success is that she achieved all of this effectively without being able to execute one of the basic strokes in tennis. Yes, you read that correctly: Graf could barely hit an attacking backhand. Much as she practised it in training, when it came to matches, she just couldn't pull it off. Fortunately, her coach got round this by making sure they spent the majority of their time in practice focusing on developing and improving her strengths: her serve, her forehand and of course her amazing footwork, which enabled her to consistently run round her backhand.

This is not to suggest that you should ignore your areas of 'weakness' entirely. Whatever you are doing, there will probably be one or two key limiters which do require you to work hard at improving them. But we need to shift the balance away from our natural tendencies. Sport shows us the benefit of playing to, and developing, our strengths. Directing our energies towards these, rather than spending so much time focusing on developing our weaknesses. Time and again I have seen the rise in people's confidence and performance from taking this approach: becoming more self-aware, recognizing strengths, understanding them and then leveraging those much more than they currently do. Focusing on them, deploying them, improving them. This provides a hugely important platform to drive confidence in your role as leader. And of course, one of the jobs of leadership is to make sure that you have people around you who add value to your team, who bring a unique contribution. As leader, you don't need to fill all the gaps – you can have someone in your team with a perfect topspin backhand.

How do you know what your strengths are? Number one: reflect. Take the time to think back through your career to date and consider what it is that you have been successful at and what has enabled it. Does your ability to inspire people stand out? Or your ability to execute on a plan in a methodical and thorough way? Your ability to focus? To listen carefully? To demonstrate empathy? Number two: ask people. Too often I see leaders held back by their concern about what people might think of them if they ask this question. Giving in to a short-term worry over something that could significantly drive long-term performance. Identify a group of trusted people whose opinion you value and ask them what they see as your strengths. Number three: take an assessment. There are a vast number of robust and insightful psychometric assessments out there that can really help you understand, and articulate, your strengths. Ask your network, get some recommendations, try a couple and read properly and digest the results.

Practise in a Purposeful Way

Knowing where to direct your effort is only half the story. The other half is the *how* – how should I harness my energy and effort in my aim to improve? What insights can sport give us in this space? This is where we turn to the remaining three elements of growth mindset: challenge, mistakes/failure and feedback.

To improve at anything, you have to 'do'. You have to jump in. You have to start trying. But you have to do this in the right way. A professional golfer doesn't just go down to the golf course and hit some balls. They will be zeroing in on particular areas to work at. They will practise specific things, in a particular way, with a specific aim in mind. And they will receive and respond to feedback (usually through a mix of coach's feedback, performance feedback and tournament feedback). This approach is commonly referred to as 'purposeful practice'. Vince Lombardi, who delivered exceptional results as head coach of the American football team the Green Bay Packers from 1959 to 1967, said: 'Practice does not make perfect. Only perfect practice makes perfect.' When aiming to improve, make sure you stretch yourself (after all, a comfort zone is a beautiful place but nothing ever grows there), be clear on what you are trying to accomplish or achieve and make sure you get good feedback. Trying and failing does not mean that you are not good enough. It means you are trying to get better and you now have even more data and insight to learn from.

It is possible, even within a busy job, to carve out time and opportunity to practise and develop particular skillsets, whether that be public speaking, listening in meetings or thinking strategically.

Where do we need to look next?

Getting Comparison Right

When it comes to real, sustainable confidence, comparison can be your enemy. But it can also be your friend. Having a growth mindset is the starting point to ensure it's your friend, leveraging comparison to improve and develop in a healthy and sustainable way. And sport, even at the elite level, teaches us something more on making comparison your friend. Even though the outcome really is about how you perform vis-à-vis your opponent.

The real comparison you should be making is with yourself. An elite athlete might well use the performance of their competitors to motivate them. They might well use it as fuel for their fire. But the best athletes and coaches also understand the need to go beyond this to ensure sustainable improvement. To focus instead on *their own* improvement.

As Grand Slam singles winner Arthur Ashe famously said: 'You are never really playing an opponent. You are playing yourself, your own highest standards, and when you reach your limits, that is real joy.'

Comparison against others can falsely increase our confidence. Or it can unhelpfully dent our confidence. If instead we focus on comparing ourselves with ourselves, on viewing our progress as against where we have been, this will drive a more tangible, substantive feeling of confidence. Yes, be aware of your rivals. Use them to drive your performance. By all means identify and keep tabs on what leadership author Simon Sinek in his book, *The Infinite Game*, refers to as 'Worthy Rivals'. But, as Sinek argues so powerfully, don't waste time and energy obsessing over them.[7]

Not forgetting the importance of consolidation

Of course if we constantly focus on learning new things, we don't leave any time for consolidation. And this is not conducive to sustained improvement. Coach Mel Marshall shared this with me at the beginning of 2021: 'People may think that my focus with Adam

---

[7] Simon Sinek, *The Infinite Game*, Penguin Business, 2019. This short video by Sinek also sets it out clearly: https://www.youtube.com/watch?v=jtpOYxsZj7o

is on continuous improvement but what I've learnt is that it is really important to periodize growth. There is a certain amount of time that you can be in your "grow zone", but unless you spend some time in your "know zone" then actually you've not consolidated and started to use the learning that you've acquired.'

Finding Your Confidence Sweet Spot

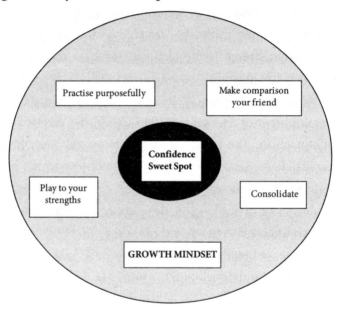

Tash was a first-time CEO. She knew she was good at her 'day job' as that was what had propelled her through the ranks but she wasn't sure if she was a natural leader, or whether she had the required skillset. She had heard of imposter syndrome and was worried that she was going to be subject to it. The chair of her new organization, knowing this was her first CEO role, suggested that Tash take on the services on an executive coach.

The coach reminded Tash that whatever we do in life we can develop and get better, provided we are committed to doing so and go about it in the right way. It's not that we can't do it, just that we can't do it YET. The coach helped Tash appreciate that no one comes fully formed. No one comes with all the attributes needed. As a first step she asked Tash to identify two areas of strength and one key limiter that would be relevant to her role. Tash did this through a combination of reflection and asking others and identified 'thinking strategically' and 'bringing people with her' as her strengths and 'being decisive' as her key limiter.

Starting with 'thinking strategically', the coach encouraged Tash to challenge herself in this area and apply this skill to the development of the new strategy that Tash was setting for the organization. The coach shared a recent *Harvard Business Review* article on strategy[8] with Tash, which examined lessons learnt from the Volkswagen emissions debacle and set out a whole new way of looking at developing strategy. The coach asked Tash to come to their next session prepared to explain to her: what she had taken from the article; what other insight she had sourced around developing strategy and what she would be taking across into the process at her organization.

In their next session, Tash delivered on this, got some great feedback from her coach on her thinking and as a result refined her ideas further. As she started the process of developing and setting the new strategy, she felt much more confident than before, knowing that she was applying and building on an existing strength.

---

[8] https://hbr.org/2017/11/your-strategy-should-be-a-hypothesis-you-constantly-adjust

In summary

- A growth mindset is key to finding your confidence sweet spot.
- The four core elements are: effort; challenge, mistakes/failure and feedback.
- A growth mindset enables you to:
  - focus on the process of improvement;
  - see failures and setbacks as iterations along the way; and
  - become comfortable with pushing yourself out of your comfort zone.
- It's not that you can't do something, it just might be that you can't do it YET.
- Playing to your strengths dramatically facilitates the process of getting the best out of yourself. Recognize them, articulate them, develop them, leverage them.
- Even in the workplace we can make time for practice and this must be purposeful.
- Concentrate on improving one skill at a time, be rigorous in your approach and remember that even 15 minutes' focused practice within your day can reap huge rewards.
- Use competition and comparison in a healthy way: competitors can spur us on, however our main focus should be on our desire to continually be better than we were the day before.
- Don't forget to allow time for consolidation – it is key.

CHAPTER TWO

How to Leave Behind Fear

'Losing is not my enemy. Fear of losing is my enemy.'

Rafael Nadal, Spanish tennis player

The year 2016 was a significant one for Lord's and for the Long Room at Lord's in particular. Lord's is owned by the Marylebone Cricket Club (MCC) and is known as the home of cricket. Established in 1787, for the first 212 years of its operation up until 1999 no women were allowed into the Pavilion (where the Long Room is situated) except cleaners, cooks and HM the Queen.

The MCC finally caught up with the times (not least due to the considerable pressure they were facing on this) in 1999 and over the first decade of this century, a handful of trailblazing women were permitted to enter the illustrious doors of the Pavilion. And it was in the summer of 2016 that this trickle of women became a temporary flood. In that famous room, which until fairly recently had still barred women, an event took place where women were the centrepiece. The room was packed full of women. The event was held during Women's Sport Week. The sponsors were Women in Sport and Investec. And the event was showcasing research which highlighted how playing sports can be beneficial for women, not only for personal health and wellbeing but also for their performance at work.

For most people in the room, the event was significant for the female angle. For me, it ended up being significant for something entirely different. I had been invited onto the panel. My fellow panellists included Dr Hannah Macleod, member of the GB Gold medal-winning hockey squad from the 2016 Rio Olympics. Macleod shared excellent insight throughout the panel session and one of the contributions that stayed with me was her revelation that she had been dropped from, or not selected for, pretty much every age-grade stage in hockey. But she had stuck at it. She'd taken on the feedback. She'd worked hard. And, importantly, she hadn't feared it. This from someone who made her international debut in 2003 and was a member of the GB team for both the 2012 and 2016 Olympics.

This message struck a chord with me. I had at the time been reflecting on the role of fear in performance, having just read James Kerr's book, *Legacy*.[9] In his book, Kerr shares 15 lessons from his time embedded with the All Blacks, the New Zealand Men's Rugby Team. The All Blacks' win/loss record makes them the most successful sporting outfit of all time, with the ratio, as I write, sitting at almost 80 per cent.

One of the chapters focuses on Expectations and how to harness fear of failure to positive effect. Like all good books, it got me thinking; in this instance about the nature of fear – where it can be positive and where it can be negative. The more I read, the more I discussed this with elite athletes and coaches, and the more I searched for answers, the clearer the message became. Fear can be useful in the short term to drive performance, but it really is not a healthy way to motivate yourself over the long term.

It's easier for many of us to gloss over fear. However, there is a danger with doing this: the adverse impact it can have on the ability to deliver consistent performance over the long term. The fear that can manifest in many different ways in leaders and which ultimately has as its root something significant that you are trying to avoid. Failing

---

[9] James Kerr, *Legacy: What the All Blacks Can Teach Us About the Business of Life*, Constable & Robinson Ltd, 2013.

in your role. Not being good enough. Not succeeding in pushing through the transformational change needed in your organization. Not reaching the numbers you need to reach this year. Not being liked. Not being *considered* good enough.

The problem with all of this is that it is draining and it means that you are focusing your energies on something negative. And it's the vital other side of the coin to the confidence sweet spot; if you don't get this right, it's going to be hard to truly stay in that sweet spot over the long term and ensure consistent and sustained performance.

So, what's the insight that we can gain from sport? What is it that's been hiding in plain sight and that can help us as leaders leave behind this significant weight?

How Do We Get This Wrong?

The seven fears in sport

Sport is a fantastic vehicle through which to view this issue, due to the focus on, and public nature of, performance. In sport, up to seven different fears have been identified as affecting performance:[10]

- fear of not being good enough;
- fear of failure;
- fear of the unknown;
- fear of being judged;
- fear of not meeting expectations;
- fear of success;
- fear of injury or re-injury.

All of these are self-explanatory except perhaps the fear of success: what this is reflecting is the fear that manifests itself when a player has

---

[10] Rob Polishook, *Tennis Inside the Zone*, Inside the Zone Publishing, 2017.

a lead and then begins to think things along the lines of 'I shouldn't be beating this person, they are ranked higher than me.' Or they may not view themselves at a certain level and therefore think they are undeserving of a victory. Other times, the uncertainty and subsequent anxiousness of putting themselves on the line for a possible victory is too much to handle. The certainty of losing, while disappointing, is well known and a familiar road already travelled.

Carrying these fears around with you is wearing. It's exhausting. And it's negative.

As two-time British Olympic fencer-turned-performance director Laurence Cassøe Halsted writes in his book *Becoming a True Athlete: A Practical Philosophy for Flourishing Through Sport*, a motivation based on fear detracts from performance far more than it benefits it. While some athletes can train themselves to master fear and continue on to great achievements, many more will quit or burn out early in their careers because the mental and emotional toll is simply too great.[11]

Now transplant this into your role as leader. One of the significant aspects of being a very good leader, in a way that is sustainable, is that you need to do all you can to look after your energy and your time. Fear can drive performance in the short term, but it can be very destructive for long-term, sustained performance. The impact on your health (physical and mental) is not sustainable. Eventually, it will out. And this has been shown even where studies have worked hard to identify any positive impact from fear. In one such study, two academics at Warwick Business School looked at how fear helps and hurts entrepreneurs. Through their research, Professor James Hayton and Assistant Professor Gabriella Cacciotti identified that fear of failure is widespread and while they were able to identify some positive aspects around motivation (centring around persistence,

---

[11] Laurence Cassøe Halsted, *Becoming a True Athlete: A Practical Philosophy for Flourishing Through Sport*, Sequoia Books, 2021, p. 35.

determination and extra effort), the negative effects were plenty, particularly around becoming less proactive and paralysis through analysis adversely affecting decision-making. Importantly, they concluded that motivation from fear can bring higher levels of stress, with potentially negative health consequences.[12]

In order to improve at your job of leadership, and perform and achieve over the long term, this negativity and focus on 'avoiding' something is not going to help. As basketball coach John Wooden famously said: 'Don't permit fear of failure to prevent effort. We are all imperfect and will fail on occasions, but fear of failure is the greatest failure of all.'

A case in point

This has been a message reinforced and acted upon by many areas of elite sport over the last few years. Not least the England Men's Football Team, where Dr Pippa Grange was brought in as a team psychologist to the players to 'make the England team fearless' with significant success. Grange has worked with an impressive array of leaders, athletes, CEOs and performers through her career. In her recent book, *Fear Less*, she describes the significant shift in her approach that occurred just over 10 years ago. She realized that real shifts weren't happening at the top of the iceberg, at the level of performance that everyone saw, but at a deeper level.[13] In her attempts to understand why some people felt unfulfilled even as they succeeded, and others felt fulfilled even in failure, she kept on coming up against the same underlying answer: fear. Fear can turn life into a constant struggle. A constant battle. And ultimately, one that will wear us out.

---

[12] https://hbr.org/2018/04/how-fear-helps-and-hurts-entrepreneurs
[13] Dr Pippa Grange, *Fear Less: How to Win at Life Without Losing Yourself*, Vermilion, 2020, p. 2, Foreword.

The link with perfectionism

Where we see the biggest issues in leaders is where fear is combined with an element of perfectionism. It's in these individuals that the desire to be perfect, amid the fear that they will not be, can have the most adverse impact on their ability to perform, consistently, over the long term.

In the introduction to this book, I referred to the Great British Medallists Research Project (*see also* page 11). The summary that I shared used words such as striving, strong work ethic, conscientiousness, commitment and achievement. All of this can bring with it shades of perfectionism. And indeed that itself is an issue in sport.

Perfectionism is viewed by many contemporary perfectionism theorists as a multi-dimensional personality characteristic comprised of two higher-order dimensions that are often labelled perfectionistic strivings and perfectionistic concerns.[14] In the context of sport, perfectionistic strivings reflect 'aspects of perfectionism associated with [athletes'] self-oriented striving for perfection and the setting of very high personal performance standards'. By contrast, perfectionistic concerns reflect 'those aspects of perfectionism associated with [athletes'] concerns over making mistakes, fear of negative social evaluation, feelings of discrepancy between one's expectations and performance, and negative reactions to imperfection'.[15]

While this area of research in the world of sport is still very much coming of age, there are some findings of real interest to the world of leadership. Perfectionist strivings are considered to be at the healthy end of perfectionism: characterized by having a self-oriented striving for excellence, high personal standards, positive reinforcement, the pursuit of realistic goals and an awareness of personal and situational

---

[14] Dunn et al., 2016; Stoeber & 65 Otto, 2006.
[15] https://ray.yorksj.ac.uk/id/eprint/4062/1/Lizmore%20Dunn%20Causgrove%20Dunn%20%20Hill%20(2019)%20PSE.pdf

limits.[16] Healthy perfectionists are able to focus on self-improvement and positive self-evaluation; and faced with challenges, they generally maintain a positive attitude, attempt to establish the reason for a failure and self-reflect in order to be able to adjust their performance in the future to avoid making similar mistakes.[17]

Perfectionist concerns on the other hand are more of a problem. They are characterized by negative reactions to and fear of failure, concern over mistakes, doubts about actions, exaggerated responses to setbacks and a chronic dissatisfaction or uncertainty about performance.[18] It hinders rather than assists sporting performance.

Linking this back with the qualities of striving and conscientiousness from the Great British Medallists Research Project, we can see that, turned to the right direction and demonstrated as perfectionist strivings, these qualities can help us achieve. And all of this reinforces a key insight: the importance of having something positive to aim for, rather than something negative to avoid. Of aligning those perfectionist tendencies towards improvement and excellence, rather than towards something that is ultimately unachievable. Of striving, in a sustainable way.

Sustaining your Performance

So, how can we leave behind fear that might be holding us back? How can we channel our efforts in a way that drives positive energy, rather than negative?

---

[16] Slade, P.D. & Owens, R.G. (1998), 'A dual process model of perfectionism based on reinforcement theory', Behaviour Modification, 22, pp. 372–390.

[17] Gotwals, J.K. & Spencer-Cavaliere, N. (2014), 'Intercollegiate perfectionistic athletes' perspectives on achievement: Contributions to the understanding and assessment of perfectionism in sport', International Journal of Sport Psychology, 45(4), pp. 271–297.

[18] Stoeber, J., Stoll, O., Pescheck, E. & Otto, K. (2008), 'Perfectionism and achievement goals in athletes: Relations with approach and avoidance orientations in mastery and performance goals', Psychology of Sport and Exercise, 9, pp. 102–121.

Allow some self-compassion

In his book referenced earlier in this chapter, Halsted highlights how important self-compassion is in helping to cope with fear. He explains that at its heart, this is about treating yourself with the same kindness that you would a close friend – to be forgiving, understanding and sympathetic and to recognize that inadequacy and making mistakes are things that everyone experiences. A bit like having an inner dialogue that resembles a combination of a kind coach and your closest teammate. Imagine if you could be more forgiving to yourself. Less judgemental. And less worried about things because you recognize that it's in the nature of humans to be flawed, not to be perfect.

Shift your focus

Once you allow in some self-compassion, it is important to try and unlock what it is that you are afraid of. If you try and ignore it and brush it under the carpet, it will linger. And it will overshadow everything you do. Whether that's through using a coach, a trusted friend, a partner or even trying to work through this on your own, opening up and unlocking the central fears that we have (and we really do all have them) is a vital first step. So, take a look at the list on page 33: which of those seven fears are relevant to you, in your role as leader? Be honest, be brave, be open.

The trick then, however, is not to wallow. Not to obsess. Not to focus too much on this, but to execute the small, subtle shift that can make a huge difference. Instead of focusing on what you are trying to avoid, what you are afraid of, **focus instead on what you are working towards**. Ask yourself, 'What is it I am aiming for? What am I moving towards?' It might be 'developing and improving as a leader' or 'being the best leader I can be'. For the

All Blacks, it has been: 'Don't just be a good All Black. Be a Great All Black'.[19]

Author and leadership expert Michelle Moore shares another strong example in her recent book, *Real Wins*. Olympic sprinter and now sports broadcaster Jeanette Kwakye was struggling to conquer her fears before the World Indoor championship 60m final in 2008 in Valencia. Her coach asked her to write the headline for the newspapers the next day. Jeanette wrote: 'Kwakye breaks British record'. Her coach then asked her to focus on the race game plan and that was it: the plan worked and Kwakye went on to claim the Silver medal in the final, breaking the British record and becoming British Champion. Jeanette had managed to release her focus on negative feelings, empowering her to break free from them and focus on a compelling and powerful positive aim.[20]

Work out what your compelling destination is and then spend your energies thinking about moving towards this, rather than moving away from something negative. While this sounds simple in theory, it is significantly harder in practice; there is no doubt though that the impact this shift has really is game-changing. The trick is to work hard on the destination; once you have come up with something, let it breathe, let it settle, come back to it and check that it works for you. That it makes sense. And that you feel confident that you can stick with it. And then reinforce it, day after day after day. As the Greek philosopher Socrates famously said: 'The secret of change is focusing all your energy not on fighting the old but on building the new.'

---

[19] James Kerr, *Legacy: 15 Lessons in Leadership*, Constable & Robinson Ltd, 2013, p. 89.
[20] Michelle Moore, *Real Wins: Race, Leadership and How to Redefine Success*, Nicholas Brealey Publishing, 2021, pp. 24–25.

Remember the Bicycle

A growth mindset is also central to coping with deep-seated fear. A growth mindset ensures that while you realize you may not be able to do something YET, if you work hard, and in the right way, you will build your ability. And if you do make a few slip-ups on the way, that is the inevitable side effect of trying to improve and get better. A growth mindset ensures that your thinking is not centred on 'being the best' or 'being talented'. This kind of thinking can quickly lead to fear of losing the label of the best or the talented one. A growth mindset ensures that you understand that you are never the finished article, that you can continue to build and develop your abilities and that putting one foot in front of the other in the right way can drive your performance over the long term. And because you believe in our ability as humans to improve and get better, you don't let fear limit your beliefs around this.

A growth mindset also ensures that you focus on the process of getting better, rather than getting too obsessed with outcomes. And particularly with outcomes that you are trying to avoid, such as not meeting expectations or not being good enough.

Beware the Dark Side of Perfectionism

'Don't let the perfect be the enemy of the good.'

Voltaire, French writer and philosopher

It's good to strive. To want to do your best. To deliver well, consistently. And it's important to continue to frame this positively. Aim for excellence. Set yourself high standards. But not impossible ones. Don't aim for perfection – this will only encourage perfectionist concerns. Turn any perfectionist tendencies towards perfectionist strivings by aligning them behind the right goal. And be aware of the situational and personal limitations. Helping you to accept that there will be times when 'good enough' is good enough.

From the field of play to the corridors of leadership

Ahmed had a very successful first stint as a CEO. He has now been poached by a much larger company, in the same sector, with some significant challenges ahead of them. Ahmed's big fear, if he's being really honest with himself, is that he won't be able to replicate his success and that his reputation in the sector will take a hit. It's taken him quite a bit of time to admit this to himself, but a conversation with a trusted mentor really helped in drawing this out. It has also helped him to realize that these feelings and concerns are normal, not something exclusive to him.

After some careful thought (and hard work on himself), Ahmed manages to shift this round in his mind. Rather than worrying about whether or not he will be good enough or 'found out', he decides to work towards doing an even better job in this leadership role than in his first one. He reminds himself that leadership is a privilege and starts to focus on what he needs to be doing to make this role a success (including not just adding new tools into his own toolbox, but also making sure he has the right people and skillsets around him).

When he has particularly challenging days, he reminds himself that he is doing his best, that he will be improving over time, even if it doesn't always feel like that. He is aware that he has perfectionist tendencies, so in his work pad that he keeps with him at all times he has the following written in the front cover: 'I am always going to strive and aim for excellence, and alongside this will remember that one of the few inevitable rules in life is that things will sometimes go wrong'.

In summary

- While fear can drive performance in the short term, it is not an effective or healthy driver for long-term, sustained performance.
- We all have underlying fears: take the time to understand what these are for you.
- Once you have done so, don't wallow in them. Shift your attention instead to what you are trying to move towards.
- If you have perfectionist tendencies, aligning them behind aiming for excellence and high standards rather than perfection will help shift those tendencies into perfectionist strivings rather than concerns.
- Take into account situational and personal limitations.
- Exercise self-compassion: channel your kind coach and closest teammate.
- Remember your growth mindset, which underpins everything.

CHAPTER THREE

How to Leverage the Power of Your Emotions

'I don't want to be at the mercy of my emotions. I want to use them, to enjoy them, and to dominate them.'

Oscar Wilde, Irish poet and playwright

Stuttgart, 2003. Chris Hoy is favourite to take the world title in the Men's 1km Time Trial, the title he first won in 2002. He's the last rider to go, and as he waits on the start line, he is prepped, primed and ready. He's in great shape. And he has a clear race plan, developed in detail with his support team.

But as Hoy waits, disaster strikes: he gets hijacked. By his own emotions. He's been watching all the other riders, and their performances have made him panic. The times have been fast. *Very* fast. He loses faith in his race plan, metaphorically throws it out of the window, and decides on an entirely different approach, involving a much faster start. All of this happens in the few seconds before he starts. The gun sounds, off he goes, tearing away, deploying entirely different tactics from the ones that he and his team had developed off the back of hours and hours of planning.

The change of plan backfires and Hoy comes in fourth. He's devastated.

After the event comes the reflection. Hoy realizes that he panicked. He had reacted to what had been going on around him. Not in a rational way but in an emotional way. And in a way that meant he had not performed as he had hoped.

Amid the disappointment, there was a significant positive to this experience for Hoy. It prompted him, despite his success to date, to realize that he could do better. That he had not got the best out of himself, even though he was already a winner. Even though he already had medals in his trophy cabinet, including a Silver medal from the 2000 Olympics in Sydney. He realized that if he was going to achieve the long-term success he wanted, if he was to achieve and perform on a sustainable basis, he was going to have to fix this problem. So what did he do? He reached out for help.

This led to the start of a long and extremely productive relationship with Dr Steve Peters, a highly respected sports psychologist who has worked with an impressive array of athletes, as well as writing a book on this area: *The Chimp Paradox*[21]. Hoy was one of the first athletes to engage the services of a sports psychologist, realizing the positive impact it could have on ensuring sustained, long-term success. His experience in Stuttgart was a wake-up call, helping him to see that he couldn't just ignore the mental side. Pretend that emotions didn't come into play. Brush them under the carpet. Instead, he realized the power of accepting that emotions do play a part in performance and of committing to developing a skillset that enabled him to leverage their power rather than letting them have an adverse and potentially debilitating impact on performance. And did he succeed? Well, as an 11-times World Champion and six-times Olympic Champion, over a career that spanned four Olympic Games, the facts speak for themselves.

Emotions drive thoughts; thoughts drive behaviour; behaviour drives performance.

---

[21] Professor Steve Peters, *The Chimp Paradox*, Vermilion, 2012.

Moments and periods of high pressure are built into the fabric of elite sport. They naturally form part of the job description. Elite sport is therefore a fantastic test bed, with lots of time and investment spent on how to get the best performance, in the moment and over the longer term, amid this pressure. Peters stated in 2012: 'My experience across various sports is that possibly as many as 90% of elite sports people will say that mental attitude and ability to deal with emotions and thoughts are critical to a successful performance.'[22]

Moments and periods of pressure are of course not exclusive to elite sport. With leadership, and in particular, senior leadership comes increased pressure. And just as in elite sport, increased pressure drives an emotional response. We all have emotions, even those who pretend that they don't. Our emotions can help our performance in leadership. They can also hinder it.

Some of the high-pressure situations commonly faced by leaders include:

- the start of a new role;
- when you know you are going to have a particularly tricky period coming up, such as when you are pushing through significant change or needing to deal with particularly complex problems;
- when you have a big industry presentation to give;
- when you are about to have a challenging conversation;
- when you are addressing your staff for the first time.

We can let the pressure get to us and get hijacked by our emotions. And suffer the resulting stress on our body. The more we let this happen, the more cumulative the damage done and the more performances

---

[22] https://www.britishcycling.org.uk/gbcyclingteam/article/gbr20120301-gb-cyclingteam-news-Managing-the-chimp---Interview--Great-Britain-Cycling-Team-Psychiatrist-Steve-Peters-0

we put in that are not equal to our potential. All of which makes it much less likely that we will stay the distance. Or, we can turn it around, learn how to use our emotions to our advantage, enabling us to achieve and sustain our performance over the long term.

How Do We Get This Wrong?

Chris Hoy's story is a powerful demonstration of how our emotions can hijack our performance. How they can cause the flight, freeze or fight response to come into play. Sport is a brilliant vehicle for seeing this in action. Known as the 'amygdala hijack' (in reference to the area of the brain that takes over in these situations), if you have ever watched a high-pressure match or competition on TV or live, you may have noticed one or all of the following:

- players can freeze – they literally look like they are operating in slow motion and often hide from the action;
- they can ask to be taken off, perhaps make more of what is a superficial injury; or
- they can turn into fight mode and deal with the pressure by becoming aggressive and overly confrontational.

For followers of football, the England men's team's humiliating exit from the 2016 Euros, losing in the quarter-final to minnows Iceland, was a perfect demonstration of a group of players getting the freeze response. The 2–1 loss represented a true nadir for the national team.

When we are under pressure, our neural activity instinctively moves away from the pre-frontal cortex area of our brain, responsible for executive planning and control, to the amygdala, which triggers our flight, fight or freeze response. This is what happened to Hoy on the start line in Stuttgart.

The same happens in the workplace. You will be able to identify at least one situation where you have had one of these responses. It's not nice. It hinders your performance and if it occurs on a consistent basis, it will have a sustained adverse impact on your ability to perform and your ability to thrive. Hoy realized that if he wanted to have consistent performance, on a sustainable basis, he needed to learn how to leverage the power of his emotions. Otherwise, if he let them hijack his performances, not only would that have consequence in the short term, the long-term wear and tear on his body and brain would hinder his ability to get the best out of himself. And it's the same in leadership. Constant suffering of the amygdala hijack is not sustainable; it impedes our ability to last the distance.

So what then are the secrets that we can learn from sport? Why is it that sports people so often repeat the phrase 'pressure is a privilege'? (Indeed, American former No. 1 tennis champion – and social activist – Billie Jean King even wrote a book with this title.)[23]

Sustaining Your Performance

Own it

The clear lesson that the field of sports psychology has shown is the importance of recognizing that emotions play a part in performance. And owning this.

Chris Hoy's story is one of many in elite sport. Just recently Dan Carter, legendary All Blacks player, shared on the High Performance Podcast[24] the fact that when he first started with the All Blacks, the focus of training was all on the physical. The consensus was that if they trained harder and longer than other teams, that would be enough. He admitted that what they hadn't realized at that time was that your emotions have a huge impact on performance. The introduction of a

---

[23] Billie Jean King, *Pressure is a Privilege: Lessons I've Learnt from Life and the Battle of the Sexes*, Lifetime Media, 2008.

[24] https://www.thehighperformancepodcast.com/episodes/dancarter

mental coach in the early 2000s changed this and led to a huge shift in the focus of their training regime. The coach, Graham Henry, ahead of his time in many respects, realized that this focus on the mental side was vital, that, in the words of the mental coach they took on, Gilbert Enoka, 'when things needed to be achieved, that the mental domain played a significant part.'[25]

Sport has learnt that emotions play their part in our performance. To accept that it's normal. To own the situation. And to build an ability to deal with it, and leverage it, in order to drive positive performances over a sustained period of time.

Hoy reached out for help. He realized this was a performance gap for him and he wasn't afraid to seek expert support. All through the lens of wanting to improve.

A simple shift in mindset

So, what's the trick? What is it that Chris Hoy and so many like him have learnt to do? The answer lies in a simple change in mindset.

Elite sport, and the sports psychologists who operate in this field, work hard at helping athletes adopt a 'challenge' mindset as opposed to a 'threat' mindset. By seeing something as a challenge, as opposed to a threat, it enables us to move our neural activity away from the amygdala to the pre-frontal cortex, which is responsible for executive planning and control. This is what Hoy needed: to move his neural activity away from his amygdala and the subsequent emotional (and, in the circumstances, irrational) response back to his pre-frontal cortex so he could execute the race plan that had been developed, agreed and practised in the build-up to the race.

---

[25] https://www.stuff.co.nz/sport/rugby/all-blacks/75526111/long-journey-for-all-blacks -mental-skills-specialist-gilbert-enoka

At its simplest, a challenge mindset is what it says on the tin: a mindset which ensures that, in situations of pressure, you view it as a challenge rather than a threat. Meaning that you are alert, ready and excited. Rather than tense, agitated and worried. Or, slightly more scientifically, an opportunity to increase your set of resources rather than an opportunity in which you may lose some of your resources.

The All Blacks articulate this in their own way, using a distinction between a Red and a Blue Head. 'Red' head is where we are tight, inhibited, results-oriented, anxious, aggressive, over-compensating and desperate. 'Blue' head is where we are loose, expressive, in the moment, calm, clear, accurate and on task. Note that this doesn't mean attempting to cancel out all emotion, more that the emotion is aligned behind seeing something as a challenge rather than as a threat.

This is backed up by some recent research out of Harvard Business School, conducted by Associate Professor Alison Wood Brooks. The experiment centred on people having to perform across various activities which generate pre-performance anxiety – maths, public speaking and karaoke singing. Some of the individuals in the study were encouraged to re-appraise their anxious arousal as excitement; the results demonstrated clearly that harnessing the arousal caused by anxiety, and using that arousal positively by turning it into excitement, had a beneficial impact on performance.[26]

So, how can we facilitate this mindset shift?

Tools we can deploy

Identify your threat mindset state

First, you need to be clear on the signs and indicators in your behaviour in order to understand when you are shifting, or likely to

---

[26] https://www.apa.org/pubs/journals/releases/xge-a0035325.pdf

shift into, a threat mindset. What are the warning signs for you as an individual when you are under pressure? Do you withdraw? Do you start operating at an even faster pace than normal? Do you start to engage in unhealthy habits or stop some of your more healthy ones? Do you find it hard to focus?

Take time to reflect on this, and try and identify what the signs are for you.

Use of language

The way we talk to ourselves, and to others, is key. Who do you think you spend most of your time talking to? Well, it might surprise you to know that, much of the time, it's yourself.

Self-talk is an accepted area of focus in the world of sport and it always amazes me that it's not more widely discussed in the field of leadership. We all spend huge amounts of time talking to ourselves and this has only been exacerbated by the COVID-19 pandemic. The language we use in our own heads, about these high-pressure situations (whether in the moment or longer-term) is central to our ability to shift ourselves into a challenge mindset.

The Harvard research referred to above reinforces this point: in the studies conducted, participants were assigned phrases to tell themselves, either 'I am calm' or 'I am excited'. Just the use of the latter phrase had a positive impact on their state of mind and their performance.

Athletes spend a huge amount of time working out what language will work for them. Performance coach Dr Dave Alred, in his book *The Pressure Principle*[27], highlights how the skilful use of language has significant influence on your ability to perform under pressure. He

---

[27] Dr Dave Alred MBE, *The Pressure Principle: Handle Stress, Harness Energy, and Perform When It Counts*, Penguin Life, 2016.

has worked with a wide variety of sports stars, perhaps most notably with Jonny Wilkinson, England rugby sensation who kicked the vital drop goal for the 2003 World Cup win. In his book, Alred explores the use of key phrases, phrases that will immediately shift your mindset. These might be ones that relate to excitement and challenge (as used in the research above) or others reminding you where to focus your thoughts and energies. Like pilots (who use Aviate, Navigate, Communicate in emergency situations), or ski-patrollers who use Assess, Adjust, Act.

Experiment. See what might work for you and then once you have honed in on a phrase, practise, practise and practise. It might even be a question that works best for you. Danny Kerry, coach of the GB women's hockey team who won Gold at the Rio Olympics in 2016, uses the following questions to help him ensure he is in the right place: 'Where am I?' and 'Where do I need to be?'[28] (Following this up with the important 'Where are they?' and 'Where do they need to be?' with respect to his players.)

Where you are facing periods of longer-term pressure, your self-talk will need to be consistent and regular. I know of many leaders who use Post-it notes or similar as visual reminders or have a book by their bedside in which they write phrases each night or each morning that help keep them in a challenge mindset. And it's not just self-talk where language is important, how you frame things to others is equally significant. If you have a challenging period coming up, do you share with lots of people the fact that you are worried and anxious about it? Or do you use language which reinforces the challenge mindset: which opens the door to the right place? 'I've got a challenging few weeks coming up; I know it will test me, I'm really

---

[28] https://www.simonmundie.com/blog/danny-kerry-self-awareness

excited to see how everything pans out and I know I will learn loads from it.'

We will focus more on language in Part Two of this book, reinforcing that when it comes to performance, to paraphrase Alred, language really is the most powerful performance-enhancing drug there is.

Aligning our butterflies

For some, this visual picture really helps. A symptom of performance anxiety is the butterflies we feel in our stomach. You can imagine them jumping around randomly or you can take the time to re-order them in your head, pushing them into a formation where they are all aligned behind the task/objective you need to achieve, excitedly waiting for the starting gun to fire. Another technique to help the shift from threat to challenge mindset.

The first sketch

Decide which emotions to keep. Your initial emotions are just that – initial emotions. Adam Grant, organizational psychologist and bestselling author, put this beautifully: 'Like art, emotions are works in progress. It rarely serves you well to frame your first sketch. As you gain perspective, you can revise what you feel. Sometimes you even start over from scratch.'[29]

It's OK to feel them. In fact, it's only natural to do so. Once you have identified these emotions, decide which ones to keep. Throw out the unhelpful ones, the ones which keep you in a threat mindset, and replace them with more helpful ones – ones that shift you into a challenge mindset.

---

[29] https://twitter.com/adammgrant/status/1302618190019727360

Threat to Challenge Mindset

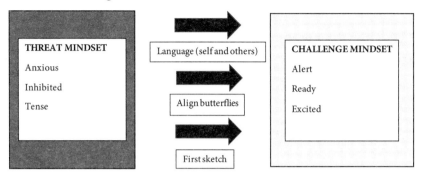

Where calm is required

Of course, not all situations are the same. There might be some scenarios where you want to be as calm as possible. Where you do want to quieten down your emotions and give yourself the best chance of performing and executing a specific, discrete task. Again, sport shows us the way. Think of moments of individual skill and pressure in sport. A penalty in football. Free throws in basketball. A bowler delivering a key ball at the sharp end of a cricket match.

Advice around breathing or giving yourself a quick break (a few minutes to step away, gain perspective, calm down) is around aplenty. And yes, these do work, often brilliantly. And there is another technique, increasingly prevalent in sport, that can also really help crack this issue: the use of anchors. I mentioned Jonny Wilkinson earlier. If you have ever seen a clip of Wilkinson kicking a penalty (and if not, do find one on YouTube now – it is so powerful), you will be aware of his pre-kicking routine. It doesn't just involve self-talk, it actually involves physical action as well. If we're honest, quite weird physical action. Why? He is using it to get himself into the required state. Anchors are a very powerful way of putting yourself in a resourceful, calm state and the process works like this: first, do just that – put yourself into a calm, positive, clear state. Then 'anchor' this state through a specific, replicable, physical action. Something out of the ordinary, like scrunching your feet or staring into the distance. Repeat, repeat, repeat until it is automatic. Then, when you are in the moment of the situation of pressure and recognize the symptoms, use the anchor to reboot and return to your resourceful state. The effect of moving your awareness to a physical sensation instead of concentrating on the pressure (and its effect), helps to distance yourself from the symptoms and calms you down quickly and easily.

From the field of play to the corridors of leadership

Etsi was six months into her role as people director. She had spent this time settling her feet under the table, getting to grips with the needs of the business and the areas where she should be focusing her time and energies. One thing was abundantly clear: things would need to change. The business was shifting dramatically in its strategy and this would require a new people structure, new systems and processes and a sweep out of the old guard. This was a first for Etsi – while she had been involved in this type of situation in previous roles, she had never led on it. She knew this was going to be challenging. She knew it would be tough. And she knew it would be lonely at times.

Etsi was worried about her ability to cope with the pressure and sustain her performance, motivation and energy throughout this period. And she was aware that she was starting to drift into a threat mindset; she was starting to get out of the habit of a daily walk, finding it increasingly hard to focus on one thing at a time at work, and she recognized that she was using increasingly negative language about the upcoming challenges when she got home in the evenings. She realized that she needed to shift her thinking: to view the upcoming period through the lens of challenge, growth, learning and doing her best rather than through the lens of worry, concern and negative anticipation. To help her with this, she put a note up on the wall in her office which read: 'This is the right thing to do. It will be hard at times but it is a privilege to be leading on it. It is exciting. Keep strong'.

Etsi found this note very useful over the subsequent months, especially on the days when things got particularly hard. And not just on her performance on each individual day, but also on her ability to perform consistently, day after day. It meant that she was finding the process much less draining than she had expected it to be, which she knew would have a positive impact on her ability to deliver and achieve over the long term.

There was one particular day, however, over which she was finding it very hard to keep a positive mindset: the day when she would be sitting down with some senior members of her team to explain the extent of the changes that were being implemented and the likely consequence on their roles. She tried hard the night before this big day to maintain a challenge mindset, with only partial success. The nerves the next morning were strong and potentially debilitating. She recognized them, identified the fact that she was feeling nervous and anxious and that she was worried about upsetting close colleagues. She then decided that these were not helpful emotions to keep at this time and so pushed them aside and instead, talked herself into a feeling of resolve, of challenge. Also, in advance of the meeting, she deployed her own anchor technique. This involved her pushing her right heel into the ground, hard, for 10 seconds. She did it just before the meeting started, and then again during the meeting when she felt her anxiety rising up again. It worked, no one noticed and she managed to keep relatively calm and composed throughout the session.

In summary:

- Emotions are inevitable.
- They can hinder your performance or help it.
- It is possible to leverage your emotions to positive effect, helping you to get the best out of yourself over the long term.
- The secret is to own the situation and leverage your emotions by moving from a threat mindset into a challenge mindset.
- Use of language is fundamental to shifting from threat to challenge – both self-talk and your articulation to others.
- Find the language that works for you and use visual reminders or other prompts to reinforce this.
- Remember your growth mindset that we looked at in Chapter 1 (*see also* pages 20–30) underpins everything – you can get better at this.
- Remind yourself when times are tough, pressure is a privilege.
- And if world-class athletes can admit that they need help and seek it, you can do the same. Isn't sustained performance in your job just as important?

CHAPTER FOUR

How to Find Sustained Motivation

'The moment of victory is too short to live for that and nothing else.'

Martina Navratilova, American tennis player

Two sisters, born just 15 months apart, into a family where no tennis had ever been played. And yet these two sisters have gone on to have the most incredible impact on this, their chosen sport. They have literally changed the game, with their style of play and approach to their professional careers flying in the face of perceived wisdom. Between them, they have won, at the time of writing (and with Serena now retired and Venus surely soon to follow, this is unlikely to change), 167 professional titles, over careers that have spanned respectively 28 and 27 years.

Yes, I am referring to Venus and Serena Williams. Venus who has won seven Grand Slam singles titles, 14 Grand Slam doubles titles (with her sister) and two Grand Slam mixed titles. And Serena with her even more impressive 23 Grand Slam singles titles, the most of any player (male or female) in the Open era. Not forgetting the 14 doubles titles, and, like her sister, two mixed doubles titles. Alongside this, they have found the time to deliver on the Olympic front as well – four Gold medals for each of them. Consider for one moment the work and effort that has gone into the prolonged success that they have both achieved. Imagine lifting a trophy 73 times (in Venus's case)[30] and 98 times (in Serena's case).[31]

---

[30] https://www.wtatennis.com/players/230220/venus-williams/bio
[31] https://www.wtatennis.com/players/230234/serena-williams/bio

What has always fascinated me is how athletes such as Venus and Serena manage to sustain their motivation. Through the success they have achieved consistently throughout their careers, what is it that has kept them continuing to put the hours in, with a relentless work ethic, when others have fallen by the wayside? And it's not only the keeping going despite success already having been achieved. It's also the keeping going when things do go wrong. Alongside their successes, both sisters will have experienced defeat more times than they care to remember. This is the case for every elite athlete, no matter how successful they are. And it's not just defeat. What about when injury strikes and an athlete has an enforced period out of the game? What keeps them going through these losses? Through the disappointment and challenging times? Along with my interest in this from a sporting point of view, as ever I have wanted to understand what the lessons are that those in leadership can learn.

I wonder how often you take the time to consider *why* you do what you do?

Imagine you have gone to a networking event. You introduce yourself to a friendly-looking person and tell them what you do. This person is quite direct and asks you why you do that job. You are taken aback but want to be polite and also give a good impression so you quickly think on your feet and you say …

Give yourself a few seconds to think what you would say. And if you'd like to, write it down. There is no right or wrong with this question. Equally, there is no doubt that to truly give of your best, on a continuing basis, among the inevitable ups and downs of leadership, in a way that ensures you can thrive and stay the distance, time taken to understand your own motivations is essential.

I always love reading the short bios of senior leaders that you see in newspapers. I particularly notice the answers to the inevitable question about whether money motivates them. More often than not you will see an answer crafted along the lines of: 'I enjoy the fact that money gives me opportunities and options, but it's not what motivates me.' What does drive them then, particularly at the level of success that most of the interviewees have achieved? What encourages them to continue to work hard? To improve and continue to achieve? And when they have a challenging patch, what motivation do they draw on to continue to strive? Let's take a look at what sport has been showing us all along.

How Do We Get This Wrong?

Outcome v mastery

It's easy to think that the world of elite sport demonstrates clearly the benefit of having a specific and compelling goal or outcome in mind. Winning the Olympics. Making the team. Achieving a Personal Best. It would seem obvious that a focus on these goals, as a way to motivate yourself as an athlete, is sensible. And yes, this is correct … up to a point. What happens though when an athlete achieves their particular goal? Or suffers a setback which makes the goal unattainable? How can they then maintain and sustain their motivation? Elite sport demonstrates clearly that despite the focus on shorter-term, concrete, tangible goals, something more is needed to drive long-term performance.

The Great British Medallists Research Project to which we referred at the beginning of this book (see also page 11) paired 32 athletes. Each of the 16 pairs comprised what was termed an elite athlete and a super-elite athlete. As well as many similarities, the study highlighted some of the distinctions between the elite and super-elite athletes. And one very clear distinction was the approach towards mastery and outcome, with a mastery focus being defined as: 'relating to mastering oneself and becoming the best I can be' and an outcome focus defined as referring specifically to winning or performing better than other people. Fourteen out of the 16 super-elite athletes reported having both a mastery and an outcome focus with respect to their sporting performance, but only three out of the 16 elite athletes. Conversely, the majority of elite athletes had a sole outcome focus: specifically, beating other people was their primary aim and this was not accompanied by an expressed desire to be the best that they could be (i.e. a mastery focus).[32]

A mastery approach ensures a primary focus on process, rather than outcome. Does this mean that athletes don't care about outcomes? Certainly not. But it does mean that they have a clear awareness of the fact that focusing on the process means the outcomes take care of themselves. This was amply demonstrated by one of the most remarkable sporting stories of 2021. In September of that year a British athlete achieved something that had not been achieved by any other athlete in her sport, worldwide. Eighteen-year-old Emma Raducanu, who just three months previously had been sitting her end-of-school exams, won the US Open tennis tournament, the first qualifier ever to win a Grand Slam. The whole run was extraordinary and Raducanu's demeanour throughout expressed her total joy at what she was experiencing, balanced with a wonderful ability to focus on each match at a time.

The approach that Raducanu and her coach at the time, Andrew Richardson, took exemplified the process-driven focus approach: not once in the five to six weeks they were in the US did they ever set a goal to win a match. Instead, they set process goals throughout the period, always learning from one to the next, all the way from qualifying through to the Grand Slam final.

---

[32] https://www.sciencedirect.com/science/article/abs/pii/S007961231730016X

Turning to someone at the other end of her career, Dame Sarah Storey is an athlete who can claim to have more to say on this than anyone. At the 2020 Tokyo Paralympic Games (held in 2021 due to the COVID-19 pandemic) she reached a career tally of 17 Gold medals, making her the most successful British Paralympian of all time. Her first Paralympics was as a 14-year-old, in Barcelona, winning five medals including two Golds[33]. Eight Paralympics later, she was not only competing but still winning Golds (Tokyo in 2021). And she has recently expressed her desire to aim for her ninth Olympic Games, Paris 2024. When asked back in 2017 about her motivation, she stated: 'It's not so much a mantra as a way of life. I choose a process-driven approach that ensures I'm searching for the best version of me. My biggest motivation is to find the peak of my physical capabilities. I hope this allows me to keep adding different stimuli and trying different approaches, alongside my tried-and-tested methods to push the personal best times and performances.'[34]

Putting this into a more every day context, imagine you have a bin in your office which sits five metres away from your chair. Not too far away, distant enough though that throwing something directly into it isn't straightforward. Your goal could be to throw your apple core into the bin. Simple. But imagine if your goal is to master the technique of throwing your apple core into the bin? To come up with the best method, and best shot ever, to land the apple core in the bin. Which of these is going to drive the more sustained effort? Not the former – once you've got the apple core in the bin, why continue? However, the latter will have you carrying out multiple attempts – at least until someone comes into your office and asks you just what you are doing.

[33] https://www.paralympic.org/sarah-storey
[34] https://www.huffingtonpost.co.uk/entry/sarah-storey-motivation-career_uk_59f098c ce4b0e064db7e1913

Mastery of course has a deep philosophical basis to it and belongs to much of the thinking in martial arts and Eastern religion. It is a topic explored in detail by co-founder and CEO of Leon John Vincent and Sifu Julian Hitch's in their book, *Winning Not Fighting*[35], where the authors examine the martial art discipline of Wing Tsun – its philosophy, techniques and application to business. The final wisdom of Wing Tsun is mastery and as Hitch explains it: 'Mastery begins by advising you to replace desiring with aspiring. You paint a picture of what you want to get, but you soften your grip on having to achieve it. By focusing on what's in front of you, you are moving towards your aspiration. As you progress, you increasingly realize that the more you give up desiring outcomes, the faster you achieve them.' As Hitch goes on to say, this indeed perhaps indicates that the universe has a sense of humour![36]

This focus on mastery is backed up by Daniel Pink in his book *Drive*. In the book, Pink examines what is the secret behind high performance and satisfaction in today's world and posits (with huge amounts of research to back it up) that there are three elements. One of them is mastery. He emphasizes that mastery is so powerful in sustaining motivation due to its elusiveness. You can approach it. You can hone in on it. You can get really, really close to it, but you can never touch it. And so mastery attracts precisely because mastery eludes.[37] So mastery is important and with this, a focus on the process to reach this rather than the outcome. And we have seen that it's something which, to the surprise of many, sport has been showing us all along.

So, what else has sport been demonstrating all along?

---

[35] John Vincent and Sifu Julian Hitch, *Winning Not Fighting: Why You Need to Rethink Success and How You Achieve it with the Ancient Art of Wing Tsun*, Penguin Business, 2019.
[36] John Vincent and Sifu Julian Hitch, *Winning Not Fighting: Why You Need to Rethink Success and How You Achieve it with the Ancient Art of Wing Tsun*, Penguin Business, 2019, pp. 360–61.
[37] Daniel Pink, *Drive: The Surprising Truth About What Motivates Us*, Canongate Books, 2011, p. 127.

Purpose

Serena and Venus Williams haven't just wanted to win a few tournaments or to be number one in the world, it's clear that they have been driven by a much bigger purpose. They have publicly stated that they have wanted to show that women can be resilient, strong and beautiful. All at the same time. And more than this, they have wanted to be role models for young black athletes in their sport. As Serena has often said, she is a black woman in a sport that wasn't really made for black people.

Developing and articulating your higher purpose is key to sustaining your motivation through thick and thin. Driving towards something that's too goal-focused, too short-term will likely mean that you come up for breath and wonder what it was all about. Yes, these can act as the scaffold, they can support and motivate you on the journey, but you are much more likely to thrive and achieve over the long term if you are working towards a higher (or as some call it, infinite) purpose.

And this lesson from sport around purpose is supported by many of the major thinkers and writers in the field of leadership and motivation. We have met Daniel Pink already in this chapter. I mentioned that in his book *Drive* he referred to the three elements that lead to high performance and satisfaction in today's world. One is mastery. And yes, another is purpose. In a post related to his book,[38] Pink quotes one study conducted by Adam Grant. Grant is an organizational psychologist, professor at Wharton and author of many excellent books himself. The study involved the call centre at a university fundraising organization. Grant obtained permission to talk to the staff working at the call centre and then randomly assigned employees to one of three groups. Some of these employees read stories from other employees describing what

---

[38] https://www.danpink.com/2010/03/is-purpose-really-an-effective-motivator/

they perceived were the personal benefits of the job, including financial benefits and the development of skills and knowledge (Personal Benefit condition). However, another set of employees read stories from the beneficiaries of the fundraising organization, who described how the scholarships they obtained from the organization had a positive impact on their lives (Task Significance condition). Finally, there was a third group of employees that did not read any stories (Control condition). In addition, the employees were told not to talk about or share what they had read with any other callers. The researcher was able to obtain the number of pledges earned as well as the amount of donation money obtained by the callers both one week prior to the study and one month afterwards.

What happened?

The results were pretty amazing. Employees in the Personal Benefit and Control groups secured the same number of pledges and raised the same amount of money as they had before the intervention. But people in the Task Significance Group, the ones who read about what their work accomplished and how it affected the world, earned more than twice the number of weekly pledges and more than twice the amount of weekly donation money.

Around the same time that Pink was formulating and sharing his insights in this area, the renowned guru in this space was developing his own body of work on the power of Why – Simon Sinek. With his book *Start with Why*[39] Simon started a movement to inspire people to do the things that inspire them. He built on this with his subsequent book *Find Your Why*[40], making the case for the importance of leaders finding their *Why*.

---

[39] Simon Sinek, *Start with Why: How Great Leaders Inspire Everyone to Take Action*, Portfolio Penguin, 2009.

[40] Simon Sinek, *Find Your Why: A Practical Guide to Discovering Purpose for You and Your Team*, Portfolio Penguin, 2017.

Sport has known this all along. For long-term, sustained motivation, you have to go beyond short-term, immediate goals towards something higher, infinite and enduring. This isn't just a new business fad, sport has been showing us all along that it's fundamental to long-term performance.

(And for those of you wondering, we will meet Pink's third element in Part Two of this book.)

Perspective

Many believe that to succeed in elite sport, you have to be totally focused. Totally single-minded. With a commitment to your sport that transcends everything else. The vast amount of anecdotal evidence would suggest that this is not the case and research is now emerging which backs this up. As Venus Williams has stated: 'To be a well-rounded person and know what's going on in the world around you, to have perspective outside of your sport, is important for every athlete.'[41]

My first direct experience of this was when I sat down in 2015 with ex-England cricketer Claire Taylor. Taylor made history in 2009 when she became the first woman to be named Wisden's Cricketer of the Year. Taylor had retired in 2011, and I was picking her brains on athlete transition. Our conversation veered into outside interests while still playing. This was because Taylor was a strong advocate of maintaining outside interests, due to the beneficial impact this had had on her cricket career. Taylor had read maths at Oxford and was also a very accomplished violinist. While early in her career she was essentially a full-time cricketer, she found that this had an adverse impact on her playing, and her mindset, and that she didn't want to be consumed by just one thing. So, she returned, part-time, to a

---

[41] Laurence Halsted, *Becoming a True Athlete: A Practical Philosophy for Flourishing Through Sport*, Sequoia Books, 2021, p. 24.

consulting day job, picked up her violin again and her performance levels literally took off.[42]

This, and so many other examples from elite athletes, led Professor David Lavallee, whom we have come across already (*see also* page 17), to conduct some research into this area. The study tracked 632 players in Australia's National Rugby League over three years and the findings showed that those who combined their sports career with time actively studying and preparing for their next career enabled them to enjoy a longer career as an athlete. As a result of the research, Lavallee anticipates that football clubs will start doing more to encourage players to develop interests outside football because of the sporting benefits, as he stated: 'This is where the performance gains will be seen within sport in the next 20 years.' Sports across the world are now taking this on board.[43]

Leadership can be all-consuming. It can be relentless. There's always something else to do, some other task to fill your time. It's a never-ending job. But if you let it take over, to the exclusion of everything else, you are unlikely to be able to maintain your motivation (and the impact on your wellbeing will most probably be severe – we will pick up on this in Chapter 6 (*see also* pages 85–99).

Celebrating Success

I often detect a level of concern in the business world around celebrating success. A reticence summed up by aphorisms such as 'pride comes before a fall'. Concern around complacency. In fact, many in sport will argue that recognizing and celebrating your progress keeps you interested. Signals where and how you are improving. Keeps you motivated. And, more than this, gives you something to

---

[42] https://www.icc-cricket.com/news/765297

[43] https://www.rlpa.com.au/fifpro-how-studying-boosts-an-athletes-sports-performance/

look forward to. Why do you think athletes celebrate big moments in matches, often with physical and verbal signals? It encourages them to keep working, to keep striving. And the emotional response associated with it provides a clear target to aim for once again. I only fully realized this on reading about Rafa Nadal's use of his 'Vamos!' ('let's go!') expression in his tennis game. The visceral way in which he celebrates big points provides an emotional marker that he continually wants to achieve and repeat.

What then can you take from these insights? What is it that you can do to sustain your motivation and so stay the distance?

Sustaining Your Performance

Ask yourself the right questions

I have found that the following questions can really help leaders understand what truly motivates them in their role. What drives them to show up, every day, trying to be the best leader they can possibly be? And what can help sustain that drive, and motivation, through all the inevitable ups and downs?

Remember, purpose isn't just for your organization. Understanding, articulating and following your own purpose are vital in ensuring that you can sustain your performance over the long term:

> *Why did I apply for this role/set up this company?*
> *Which are the aspects of my job that bring me joy?*
> *Which are the aspects of my job that I'm really good at?*
> *What are the aspects of my job that I try and avoid?*
> *What do I want people to say about my leadership once my stint is up?*
> *What are my aims and ambitions for this organization during my leadership?*
> *Did I take on this role for a wider purpose? If so, what? What's the change that I want to see in society?*

What's the impact I want to have beyond my organization?
What have I still got left to achieve?
What setbacks have I encountered in my career to date? And what have
they led to?

All of this can help maintain your motivation and articulate your higher or infinite purpose.

Mastery: Focus on the process

Work on the process of developing and improving your leadership. Make this your focus, aim to 'master' leadership and the outcomes will take care of themselves. Hone in on particular areas. Set yourself some process goals. Identify the areas you want to work on (remembering to give sufficient weight to developing your strengths). Free yourself to experiment and try new approaches, just like Sarah Storey. Use the principles of purposeful practice that we explored in Chapter 1 (*see also* page 26). Remember the bicycle, and aim to get better over time.

Mastery Approach

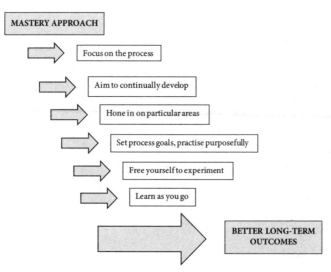

Perspective

Former British prime minister Winston Churchill wrote in 1965: 'The cultivation of a hobby and new forms of interest is a policy of first importance to a public man.'[44] While I would take issue with the female exclusion from this quote, this will inevitably have been correct at the time he was writing. The point that he makes though is an important one: keep an eye on other areas of your life and ensure they don't get left behind. I once heard a senior recruitment consultant state that he measured CEOs and their ability to keep perspective by hearing accounts of how they spent their weekends. How do you spend yours? Do you switch off? Focus on other things? Get busy with hobbies and family? Or do you mostly work?

Celebrate your successes

While you may be good at making sure your organization celebrates success, make time to do so for yourself as well. At the end of 2021, after a particularly hard and challenging year, one CEO with whom I had been working wrote down the list of all that she had achieved that year. The list was much longer than she had initially anticipated and was a significant lever in maintaining her motivation and re-energizing her for 2022. It doesn't have to be big and public, do it in a way that suits you whether that's some quiet personal reflection time or a meal out with those closest to you.

---

[44] Winston Churchill, *A Man of Destiny Winston S. Churchill*, Country Beautiful Foundation Inc., Winsc., 1965.

From the field of play to the corridors of leadership

Tom has been managing partner at his law firm for four years. In general, he gets a real buzz from his job, however he has had a particularly challenging time over the last 18 months. He's been trying to drive huge change through his firm. This has led to a significant number of issues and an incredibly full diary. At times Tom has got quite close to feeling overwhelmed and in his most challenging moments has asked himself the questions 'Is it really worth it? Should I really be continuing in this role? Am I making the difference I wanted to make?'

He has always been pretty good at keeping his job in perspective, helped by family life and his hobby, cooking. But what he's feeling now seems more deep-seated. Over the next few weeks he makes a conscious effort to think through what he enjoys about his role and why he's doing it. He finds the time to walk and think, the time to discuss with trusted people in his network and the time to discuss with his partner. Through this process he realizes that his role as managing partner has given him an opportunity to make a difference far beyond the day job of helping his clients. Through the changes he is driving in his firm, he is improving the culture, improving the experience of the people in the firm and providing increased opportunity for them to fulfil their potential. This is what is really motivating him. This is what he really cares about. With this realization, Tom finds renewed energy and purpose in his role, with a focus now on seeing through the changes he has instigated in order to really drive the benefits that he knows will flow. He has also come to realize that great leadership isn't so much about the destination as it is about the journey; that of continually trying to improve and develop, and 'master' it. He knows that a central plank of the change he is trying to create is in ensuring strong and robust succession planning, so sets out with renewed energy to try and master this area in particular, leveraging his naturally methodical and thorough approach to the planning and goals that ensue.

In summary

- Focus on mastery – and the <u>process</u> of continually trying to improve and develop rather than outcomes.
- If you do this properly, the outcomes will take care of themselves and you will have a better chance of maintaining your motivation through the inevitable ups and downs.
- Understanding your own purpose is central to maintaining your performance and commitment over the long term. Make the time to identify this.
- Keep perspective – make sure you have something in your life that takes you away from the day job.
- And do make sure you celebrate success; it provides an important marker in the sand, as well as something to strive for again.
- Remember your growth mindset from Chapter 1 (*see also* pages 20–30) – this underpins everything.

CHAPTER FIVE

How to Bring the Required Discipline to the Table

'Keep working, even when no one is watching.'

Alex Morgan, US soccer player

Alex Danson was leading goalscorer of the GB women's hockey team that won Gold at the Rio Olympics in 2016. We will hear more of the team's story later in the book, but for now we will focus on Danson. Danson was one of the athletes interviewed by world-beating triathlete Alistair Brownlee in his recent book *Relentless: Secrets of the Sporting Elite*.[45] The book is fascinating thanks to the selection of athletes whom Alistair interviews and the insight and perspective shared as a result of Brownlee's tenacious, open-minded and broad interest in what drives performance. The interview with Danson reinforced what so many in elite sport know: while talent is only the starting point, the often-quoted next step, motivation, still doesn't provide the whole answer. What else is required? Discipline.

In the book Danson states: 'I've always believed that the most talented people aren't the most successful; it's the workers, the ones who want to achieve something a little bit more than the next. In our case, the last to leave the training session or the one that's willing to go and do the training when no one's looking.' She went on to say:

---

[45] Alistair Brownlee, *Relentless: Secrets of the Sporting Elite*, HarperCollins Publishers, 2021.

'extraordinary people are not born – extraordinary people are made. And they're made by doing the simple things repeatedly.'[46]

Reinforcing this point is the author of another book called *Relentless*, this time with the subtitle *From Good to Great to Unstoppable*. This author is Tim Grover, an international authority on sports performance and motivation. He has worked with many of the all-time basketball greats such as Michael Jordan and Kobe Bryant. In his book Grover shares his beliefs, and the elements of his approach, around greatness. Once again he puts the spotlight on an issue that so many of us miss. Motivation in itself is not enough; to truly improve, develop and achieve over the long term, discipline is the vital other side of the coin. You have to turn motivation into action and results.

As he notes in the introduction to his book, discussing Kobe Bryant: 'It takes years of tireless dedication and unimaginable hard work to build a legacy like Kobe's.'[47] Indeed in all the studies that have been done looking at what it is that sets elite athletes apart, there is one element that is pretty consistent across the board and that is the ability of elite athletes to put up with the drudge. To train hard. To work hard. To do all the small things. Over and over again. To a level at which most of us would have got fed up a long time ago. The ability to consistently and relentlessly cover the basics, focus on the key components and push themselves on these. Even when they're not feeling it.

One of the first studies to pick up on this was a study by Daniel Chambliss called 'The Mundanity of Excellence' (such a great title!) In the study, conducted between 1983 and 1984 (with his paper being published in 1989), Chambliss examined, via research among elite swimmers, what role talent plays in excellence. He defined excellence

---

[46] Ibid, p. 99.

[47] Tim S. Grover with Shari Lesser Wenk, *Relentless: From Good to Great to Unstoppable*, Scribner, 2014, p. xi.

as consistent superiority of performance. His study found that there were three core dimensions of difference: technique; discipline and attitude. The best swimmers were more disciplined in their approach and they cultivated better habits. Not only this, but the aspects that the lower-quality swimmers found arduous or boring, such as 'swimming back and forth over a black line for two hours' created much more positive reactions in the top-level swimmers, where they actively enjoyed and looked forward to the hard practices.[48]

Your motivation is what drives you but that's not the whole story. You need to bring determination to the party as well, ensuring that you demonstrate the discipline required to perform over a sustained period. Because there will be days when, no matter how strong your motivation is, you're just not 'feeling it'. Days when, in the words of the renowned expert in this field, B.J. Fogg, you are very much at the bottom of your motivation wave.[49]

What's true for sport is true for leadership. Where we see sustained improvement and performance in leadership is where people can put the daily grind in. To keep working, even when no one is watching. This is fundamental to sustained performance in leadership and the ability to thrive. It's all very well knowing what you should be doing, and understanding why, but you have to actually do. Consistently. Over the long term.

How Do We Get This Wrong?

Behaviour change theory helps us understand why discipline, on top of motivation, is key to sustained success. And how and why things can go wrong. Most theories of behaviour change tend to focus on three core elements: what you need to do, why you need or want to

---

[48] https://academics.hamilton.edu/documents/themundanityofexcellence.pdf
[49] https://behaviourmodel.org/motivation/

do it and how to make it more likely than not that it's actually going to happen.

One of the best articulations of these elements is provided by American authors Dan and Chip Heath in their book *Switch: How to Change Things When Change is Hard*.[50] To represent the different elements in any behaviour change, they use the image of an old-fashioned colonial rider sitting atop an elephant, trying to make their way towards their destination. The rider equates to what they (and many) call our rational brain. The bit that needs clarity, instruction and guidance – the 'what' of behaviour change. The elephant equates to what they call our emotional brain – the powerful element that's actually motivating us to do something, linked to our desire and our willpower. In other words, the 'why' of behaviour change. And their nudging element, the bit that makes the good behaviour more likely to happen, they call Shaping the Path.

Picture it. A rider, sitting on top of an elephant, with a nice easy path to follow. You can now use this image to conjure up a visual reflection of the key barriers to driving certain behaviours. No matter how much the rider might be aware of what the outcome needs to be, if their elephant is not motivated to get there, it's not going to happen. Similarly, no matter how motivated the elephant is to get to the destination, if the rider doesn't know how to get there, it will simply be churning up the ground in the same spot. Even where both rider and elephant are ready to get going, if the terrain is obstructive, getting to the destination will be extremely hard, meaning the rider and elephant are more likely to give up.

The elephant is the most powerful element in this narrative and this is why the examination of motivation in the previous chapter (*see also* pages 57–71) is so important. And why the discussion on growth

---

[50] Chip and Dan Heath, *Switch: How to Change Things When Change is Hard*, Random House Business Books, 2011.

mindset also underpins all of this – helping you understand that progress is not linear, that there will be setbacks, and ensuring you can maintain your motivation in the face of these. Alongside this, the rider of course needs to be clear on the destination and the best way to go about getting there. So you need to be able to direct your rider.

Let's see how this works in practice, using the example of Sandra the skateboarder. Sandra has aspects that she needs to work on. These are her kick turns and mindset. Kick turns because this is already a significant weapon for her as a skateboarder and so one to consolidate and leverage even more. Mindset because for Sandra it is a weakness and something that has a fundamentally negative effect on her performance and enjoyment. She has clear rules and processes in place for how to develop each of these aspects, helped by her coach.

Sandra has the clarity needed to direct her Rider. And she's doing all of this because she wants to be the best skateboarder she can be, with a specific goal of winning her local skateboard competition in nine months' time. So that's her Elephant sorted. But if she doesn't have the required discipline to put this into practice, day after day after day, all this motivation and clarity won't get her to where she needs to be. And so we come to the final element in behaviour change, the one that gets to the crux of discipline: how we shape the path. How do we make it easy to put the work in? Day after day after day? How do we make the good behaviour easy and the bad behaviour hard?

One way is to tweak our environment. If I'm trying to lose weight, then tweaks might include: keeping only the right foods in the house, using smaller plates for meals. If I'm trying to go to the gym more often on my way into work, packing my bag the night before and leaving it by the front door will help. For Sandra, changing her chosen skate park might make all the difference – the new park is packed with determined, innovative, ambitious, hardworking skaters who are all aiming high, just like her.

For those in elite sport, ensuring their environments support their ability to bring a disciplined approach is fundamental. Whatever sport, whatever national league, elite clubs will do all they can to provide an environment that supports performance. From the layout of the gym via the weekly routines and schedule, right through to the food provided in the canteen.

Another tool to shape the path is the building of habits. Habits enable us to do things on autopilot, without having to spend time and energy thinking about them. James Clear has written extensively on how to build effective habits, in particular in his book, *Atomic Habits*.[51] One of the techniques he advocates is that of habit stacking, a concept originally devised by B.J. Fogg, whom we came across earlier (*see also* page 75).[52] We know that on top of our existing neural pathways, we create new ones all the time. And that these pathways become faster and stronger every time we do something; this is the essence of skill development. Building new habits takes time and habit stacking seeks to take advantage of existing connections and stack your new behaviour on top. Thereby making it much more likely to happen and stick. For example, after I pour my cup of coffee each morning, I will do five press-ups. Or after I finish dinner every evening, I will call my mother.

For Sandra, this is an easy one. She has an already established habit which is that the last thing she does before finishing every training session is five kick turns. She's now going to stack another habit on top: before she leaves every training session, and after the kick turns, she's going to spend five minutes on one of her mindset exercises.

And it's these habits, committed to day after day after day, that make the difference. It's this disciplined approach that enables you to truly improve, perform and achieve on a sustained basis. This is what

---

[51] James Clear, *Atomic Habits*, Random House Business, 2018.
[52] https://jamesclear.com/habit-stacking

athletes such as Alex Danson mean when they talk about doing the small things, repeatedly, even when no one is looking. This consistent behaviour, these consistent habits, are what ultimately drives long-term, sustained success.

Knowing what it is you need to be doing, and being motivated to do so, only gets you so far. If you don't build in the habits, maintain the discipline, keep working when no one's looking in a way that becomes automatic, then no matter how motivated you are, your Elephant will likely veer off. Sport has been showing us this all along. And sport has been showing us something more: that if you can not only get to a place where the grind is easy, but where you actually enjoy it (think back to Chambliss' swimmers, *see also* page 74), this is where your performance over the long term will really fly. So how can you take this understanding of discipline across into your leadership?

Sustaining your Performance

As with sport, improving and developing as a leader takes determination. It takes hard work. It takes discipline. And it takes a focus on small and consistent behaviours, day after day after day.

'We are what we repeatedly do. Excellence, then, is not an act but a habit.'

Aristotle

Tweak your environment

Just as elite athletes and their coaches realize the importance of having an environment around them that gives them the best chance of sustained success, so should you as leader. Does your working environment help or hinder your performance? Does it encourage too many distractions or help keep them out? What prompts and nudges do you have in place to ensure relentless discipline on the behaviours and tasks that matter? How are you tweaking your environment to give yourself the best chance of improving and developing?

By way of example, imagine that in my leadership role I feel that I need to get better at listening. I am motivated to do so because I've had quite a lot of feedback that suggests that it's something that is holding me back. I recognize and believe that developing this skillset is going to help me fulfil my potential as leader and produce the outcomes I and my organization would like to see. I've had some useful advice about how to do it, one of which is the five chip approach. This was explained to me as follows: in any appropriate meeting that you attend, imagine you have five chips. Every time you speak, that's one of your chips gone. Once you've used up all five, you can't make any further contribution to the meeting.

I see this as a very valuable practice technique, despite the fact that I know it will feel a bit awkward and uncomfortable to start with. I also understand that if I don't make it as easy as possible to do, it's unlikely that I will start, let alone continue. Meaning that I will fail in my attempt to develop my skillset around listening.

I know I have to tweak my environment. First of all, I reflect carefully on what meeting I should start to practise this in. I decide that my weekly leadership team meeting, with my fellow executive directors, is the right forum. At the next meeting I share with them some of the feedback I have had and explain what I am going to be practising accordingly. I also actually bring five casino chips with me (from our family poker set) and put them on the table in front of me. Each time I speak, I put the chip into the middle of the table. On the odd occasion that I forget, my colleagues remind me to do so.

Think how much more likely these actions are to drive improvement in my listening skills. I have tweaked my environment to give myself a much better chance of success and the more I do this, the more

I practise, the more I focus on these small changes to build this skill-set, the more likely it is that not only will I improve my performance in this area, but I can start to take enjoyment from the process.

Build in habits

How can we use habits to help? Imagine I want to get better at taking a more structured approach to my working day. Let's say that I currently start my working week with a half-hour call with my team. This takes place at 8.30 a.m. After this, I tend to rush straight into tasks and get so caught up that I forget to plan and prioritize. I know this is detrimental and something that I need to change. As I already have a habit set (the team call at 8.30 a.m. on a Monday morning), I decide to stack another habit on top of this: at the end of each team call, I will block out 30 minutes in my diary. I will use this time to do some planning for the week, with a focus on priority tasks that need to be accomplished. I sit at my desk and block this time out for the remaining weeks of this calendar year and also ask my assistant to help me ringfence this time.

A simple habit, stacked upon one I already have, with a couple of tweaks to make sure it happens. That might, in an ideal world, become something that I enjoy. Not a grind. But a task in which I take pleasure. Because I recognize how important it is to my long-term success.

Be consistent in your behaviours

What this means is that we can then be consistent in our behaviours. It's just like going to the gym. If you want to be strong and fit over the long term, then a short burst of intense gym-going, followed by a swift drop-off due to the lack of thought into what approach is going to work best is not going to help. But if you're clear on why you want to get fit and strong, give yourself some clear aims and components in your programme AND build habits and tweaks that drive consistency in your behaviour, you're giving myself a much better chance. And these behaviours then become automatic. No longer new, or too difficult, or too daunting, they are just part of your daily routine, part of what makes you *you* and instrumental in your ability to perform, develop and improve on a sustained basis. And, in an ideal world, things you actively look forward to, knowing the benefits they give, just like Daniel Chambliss' top-level swimmers.

From the field of play to the corridors of leadership

Fola has been in her current CFO role for seven years. Before that she was CFO at a different and slightly smaller corporate. She now acts as a mentor to aspiring leaders in her sector. One of them recently asked her how she managed to keep going. To keep up her schedule, and continue to perform, over such a long period of time. Fola shared how important discipline had been. She explained that she had always been ambitious and always wanted to achieve. Quite early on in her career she had realized though that in order to get to where she wanted to get to, she had to build some good habits and give herself the best chance of maintaining them.

One of these habits is that at the end of each week, she looks back over her weekly to-do list and makes sure that, barring real emergencies, everything is ticked off. She has also, since being CFO, consistently maintained her habit of always being the last to speak in team meetings when a point for discussion has been raised. A simple and basic approach, it has been invaluable in making sure that as the most senior person in the room she is not dominating or influencing the discussion. It has got to the point now where these, and other habits and behaviours she has built in, are no longer a nuisance or a chore, but things she gets real pleasure from doing.

Fola also shared the fact that very occasionally she did find herself 'falling off the wagon'. Letting some of her fundamental habits and behaviours slip. But she had good tripwires in place to watch out for this (for example, if her inbox hits over 50 emails still waiting to be dealt with, this is a warning for her to get back on top of it) and recognized that no one is perfect. This helped her in understanding that a slip-up wasn't terminal, but something much more to be viewed as a temporary blip, thereby helping her get back on track.

In summary

- Discipline is an essential component to long-term success.
- Shaping the path in the right way gives you the best chance of bringing the required discipline to the table.
- The 'good' behaviours need to become easy and automatic.
- Make the right tweaks to your environment. Build some simple habits. They do not need to be complicated.
- Discipline then becomes just part of your daily routine from which you may even learn to find joy.
- Find what works for you. And repeat. Repeatedly.
- And remember your growth mindset from Chapter 1 (*see also* pages 20–30) – this underpins everything.

CHAPTER SIX

How to Prioritize Your Time

'Time is relative; its only worth depends on what we do as it is passing.'

Albert Einstein, theoretical physicist

Jessica Ennis-Hill has a superpower. Ennis-Hill was the face of her home Olympics, London 2012. Favourite to win the heptathlon, everywhere you looked in the build-up to the Games, her face was there. Young, athletic, photogenic, positively brimming (at least in the photos) with confidence and belief. Imagine the pressure. Imagine the expectation.

And Ennis-Hill coped with it brilliantly. She won Gold on what became known as Super Saturday, the day on which three British athletes won Gold: Ennis-Hill, Greg Rutherford (long jump) and Mo Farah (10,000 metres). Everyone I know who was in the stadium at the time rates it as one of the top three moments in their life. (Sadly, I was not there!) But this is not the superpower to which I'm referring, it's what this was built on: her ability to prioritize her time.

Ennis-Hill was always known as an athlete who was incredibly focused. One who was able to turn up, switch on, commit and then leave the track and move on to something else. This ability was tested dramatically after the birth of her son, Reggie, in 2014. Having made the decision to come back and aim for Rio 2016, Ennis-Hill had to become even more focused and disciplined over her use of time, fitting in her training schedule around her young son. And how did she do? Well, she won a second World Title in 2015 just 14 months after Reggie was born and won a hugely impressive Silver in Rio in 2016.

And she's not the only athlete with this superpower. This ability to prioritize time in a way that enables athletes to achieve astonishing success over prolonged periods of time, despite the relentless slog of professional sport and all the other demands on their time, is demonstrated by so many. What enabled Roger Federer, winner of 20 Grand Slam titles, to extend his career to 41 years of age? What enables Rafa Nadal, winner of 22 Grand Slam titles at the time of writing, to still be going strong at 36 years old? And what about Tom Brady, widely considered to be the greatest quarterback of all time, who is playing a 23rd season at the age of 45?

Every professional athlete has the same number of minutes in each day, the same number of days in each week and the same number of weeks in each year. It's how they use that time that's critical. And it's why the ability to prioritize, the ability to use those minutes, days and weeks in the best way possible is central to the ability to perform at a high level, over a sustained period of time. To avoid burnout. To avoid being distracted by things that will hinder not help performance.

The athletes mentioned above, and so many others like them, take an extremely focused approach to how they use their time. Knowing what will help, and what will hinder, in their determination to improve, perform and achieve over the long term. Leaders need to develop the same skillset. To ensure that they can perform, and thrive, over a sustained period of time. And it's even more important in leadership as your career does not need to be cut short early due to the march of time on your physical prowess and capabilities, unlike those of elite athletes.

While the relentless developments in technology are generally presented as beneficial in terms of effective use of our time, we all know that the reality is that it can get harder and harder to really focus our time. To compartmentalize. To be clear on what needs doing, now. And to properly switch off when needed. You might be thinking that it's easy for athletes to be good at this. Their job is relatively simple: train and then perform. But of course the reality is that the more successful an athlete becomes, the more they accomplish, the more demands they have on their time. Sponsorship deals and commitments, broadcasting requests, appearances and openings, to name just a few. So, what is it that we can learn from these elite sports people? Those who really do stay the distance, despite the demands on their time.

How Do We Get This Wrong?

What does my job actually involve?

As a leader, the chances are that you have a pretty well-developed skillset. There's probably quite a lot of what goes on in your organization or division that you are more than capable of doing. And it's important to keep your hand in, after all. You also know that you need to give time and space for the people side of things. You probably also have an external role to play in some shape or form. You can see that you are just going to get busier and busier but that's OK – leaders are meant to be really busy, you owe it to your organization …

Right?

No. Fundamentally wrong.

As a leader, your time is the most important asset you can give to your organization. This means that it is a key strategic asset for your organization. And, following the laws of economics, there is an opportunity cost involved with every minute that you spend on something. Your main responsibility is to make sure that you are spending your time in the right way, on the right things. And in a way that means that you can sustain your performance (and success) over a prolonged period of time.

What I often find is that leaders approach the beginning of their tenure with an enthusiastic, keen and rapacious approach. Saying yes to many things. Not having complete clarity on what they should, and should not, be spending their time on. That can be manageable for the first couple of years. And then they tend to see what I call the 'tsunami' impact, where all this work suddenly produces a seismic and overwhelming wave of work and commitments. Acutely and adversely impacting on their time. Their wellbeing. And their performance. And this is not a good place to be in.

I wonder if you have you ever sat down and categorized what your role involves? What are the key areas to which you need to devote your time? If you haven't, why don't you do it now? Perhaps grab a piece of paper and write down the list.

How many areas have you got? Of course every leader's job will differ slightly, however there are usually some consistent themes that come out:

- strategy;
- culture;
- external stakeholders; and
- people.

Quite how these are framed will depend on the type of organization you work in and/or lead. For example, if you lead a large organization, the people element will probably revolve predominately around working with your leadership team. It might also include working with your Board. The strategy focus would usually be setting rather than implementing.

What can help you come up with the right list for you and your organization? A brilliant rule of thumb is to follow the advice from Microsoft's only third-ever CEO – Satya Nadella. He once said: 'One of the things we sometimes confuse is all the things we should be doing versus all the things only you could do.'[53] So think about what's important, think about who can do what and specifically consider: what are the things that only you can do? This is where you should be spending your time. Of course, with this comes the necessity of building your ability to say no. If you can't do this, you are not going to get very far with the task of doing what only you can do. We will pick up on this later.

Managing your energy

Elite sport has understood for some time now that, rather than being opposite ends of the spectrum, wellbeing and performance are inextricably linked. Lizzie Simmonds is an ex-GB swimmer who now serves as chair of the Athletes' Commission at the British Olympic Association. She wrote in 2021, in a blog exploring just this issue: 'Ask any athlete in the world and they will tell you that performance and wellbeing are not mutually exclusive; they are, in fact, entirely symbiotic. It is not possible to perform to your best in a sustainable way if you are not prioritising your mental and physical health. Wellbeing is not fluffy; it is the foundation of high-performance.'[54]

---

[53] https://www.fastcompany.com/90425588/satya-nadella-on-learning-listening-and-his-1-productivity-hack
[54] https://lizziesimmonds.com/2021/09/16/wellbeing-vs-performance/

Wellbeing's relationship with Performance

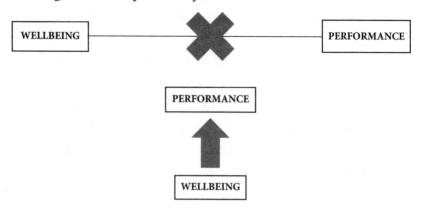

For long-term, sustained success, you have to get this right.

In early 2021, McKinsey & Company published an article titled 'The Mindsets and Practices of Excellent CEOs'. In it, the authors set out the six main elements on which they believe every CEO, regardless of size and sector, should be spending their time. Amid the expected (strategy, external relationships and so on), one of the six was managing one's own time and energy.[55]

Why is this important?

There is a myth, popular in the professional services world in particular (although thankfully, even this is changing now), that good leadership equates to long hours and constant work. I hear a common refrain along the lines of: 'I'm so busy I haven't got time to exercise/take time off/think of myself/go for a walk each day/breathe ….' This is entirely misguided and generally prompts barely concealed frustration from me. I recommend (and urge) a small yet significant shift in mindset: 'I am so busy that **I must** find time to exercise/take time off/think of myself/go for a walk each day/breathe ….' We all

---

[55] https://www.mckinsey.com/business-functions/strategy-and-corporate-finance/our-insights/the-mindsets-and-practices-of-excellent-ceos

know that we operate best when we are feeling strong, when we are feeling relatively rested and when we are building in time to check in with our mental and physical health. A leader is responsible for a lot of people and a lot of outcomes so give yourself the best chance of ensuring this – it really is a marathon and not a sprint.

Sport obviously shows us the way in terms of the focus on areas such as nutrition and sleep. And these are of course equally as important in your role as leader if you want to stay the distance. But that path has been fairly well trodden. What has been more hidden is the lesson from sport around smaller changes and we can turn to some research from the world of tennis to find out more.

Micro breaks

In the early 1990s, Dr James Loehr – a respected sports psychologist, author of *The Power of Full Engagement*[56], and the founder of the Johnson & Johnson Human Performance Institute in Orlando, Florida, conducted some research on elite tennis players. Loehr wanted to understand what it was about the top tennis players, who consistently delivered in the big tournaments, that set them apart. Why, despite the fact that there were hundreds of players on the international circuit, only a handful of champions consistently brought home the trophies. What was it that these elite did differently from the other, equally talented tennis players? Loehr performed all sorts of analyses and much to his frustration, couldn't find any consistent differences among the top players – until he started looking at what they did *between* points. And a pattern jumped out immediately. After examining countless hours of video, he noticed that these top players exhibited very similar habits between points

---

[56] Jim Loehr and Tony Schwarz, *The Power of Full Engagement: Managing Energy, Not Time Is the Key to High Performance and Personal Renewal*, Simon and Schuster, 2005.

and in the changeover between games. And these habits were focused on saving energy and ensuring a positive focus.

Through the use of heart-rate monitors, he discovered that these players were able to bring their heart rate down to an ideal zone more efficiently than the less successful players and the further he went down the list of seeded players, the more significant the differences were. Loehr used this discovery to revolutionize the training on this and now it is commonplace to see players turning their backs to the court after each point, picking up their towel, gathering themselves and then getting back in the zone for the next point. Similar behaviours take place at changeovers.[57]

Periodizing your effort

Sport also has some useful insight to show in terms of managing your energy through the year. Jessica Ennis-Hill, like all athletes, will have had points in the season where she needed to peak. Periods where she needed to build in some downtime and periods where she needed to put the hard yards in. And this is no different from the rhythms and patterns that many senior leaders encounter, such as school leaders, anyone involved in publicly listed companies or companies that have attracted private equity or venture capital funding. You need to learn how to find your way through these requirements in a way that ensures you can continue to ride the waves and perform over the long term.

Tennis is a particularly good example here. Like most sports, the professional tennis tour (men's and women's) has a flow to it. The same tournaments take place in the same weeks in each calendar year. Each season there is a relentless list of tournaments. Players need to

[57] Bonnie St. John and Allen Haines, *Micro-Resilience: Minor Shifts for Major Boosts in Focus, Drive and Energy*, Piatkus, 2017, pp. 9–10.

take part to build their ranking points. The higher their ranking, the more likely they are to be seeded, which as a general rule makes their progress through tournaments slightly easier, thereby increasing their chances of continuing to improve their ranking. All of which builds towards tournament wins and with this the increase in prize money and sponsorship deals that flow. Players need to pick and choose their entries, and their training blocks, accordingly. Too many tournaments without a rest and they run the risk of injury or burnout. Too few and they reduce the chances of peaking and performing well at the big tournaments. They need to time their effort, in a strategic way. Rest and recovery blocks are planned as part of the performance cycle, with the recognition that they are central to long-term performance.

What is it then that all of this points to in terms of how to sustain your performance? What lessons can we learn and deploy as leaders?

Sustaining Your Performance

Clarity on your role

Spend time gaining clarity on what your role actually involves. What are the elements that you need to be working on to achieve what you need to? And what actually is your role in these elements? For example, leading the top team might be one. But what does this actually look like? What is it that this actually requires from you?

One way to help you understand your core areas is to do a diary audit. Once you have drawn up your categories of areas of responsibility that fall within your remit, take a look back at your diary over the last two weeks and overlay your categories. How much of your time was spent outside of your core areas? If it's 5 per cent, you are doing very well. If it's 30 per cent, you have a problem. Either you need to redraw your list, or (if you are confident your current list is correct), you need to let go of this extra stuff. Distil it down, categorize it and move it on to someone else.

Building your 'saying no' muscle

'Saying no is not letting others down. It's standing up for yourself. Setting boundaries isn't a display of disrespect. It's an expression of self-respect. Other people can't set your limits. They have the right to make requests, but self-preservation is your responsibility.[58]

Adam Grant

A fundamental outcome of being clear on your priorities is clarity on what you should be saying no to. Once you have your list of categories that need your time and attention, and once you are clear on what this looks like in practice, you will have a much better understanding of what your role does not involve. What you should NOT be spending your time on. That's the first step.

The second step is of course having the confidence and ability to do so in the right way.

Rules and prompts

In this case, rules and prompts can help significantly. Some leaders I have worked with have a sheet up by their work station, setting out their role and areas of responsibility. This can act as a brilliant prompt to remind them what they should and should not be doing, applying the rule: 'Does what I am about to do/agree to fit within my categories of work?'.

In terms of saying no, some people, particularly those who find it hard to do so, have a 'saying no' script in which they ensure that it is done politely, with respect and ideally ensuring that the recipient of the 'no' understands their reasoning.

---

[58] Adam Grant, Twitter, 27 October 2021

Pause

Another technique that you many find useful is that of building in a pause. Developing this habit can be incredibly useful, particularly for those who tend to be people pleasers. For those who find it hard, in the moment, to disappoint someone. Asking someone to give you 24 hours before you give them your response enables you to go away and reflect properly on the request instead of giving in to a gut response or fear of upsetting someone.

Gatekeeper

Make sure you have the right gatekeepers around you. The most effective leaders I have worked with have a strong relationship with their support team and provide them with absolute clarity on areas of priority and responsibility, and what should come through to them and what should not. As noted in the McKinsey & Company article I have already referred to (*see also* page 90): 'The most successful CEOs quickly establish an office that makes their priorities explicit and helps them spend their scarce time doing work that only CEOs can do.'

Letting go

In order to focus on what it is that only you can do, you also need to develop the ability to let go. Letting go can be hard. The tendency for many leaders at times can be to get involved in areas that they should not be. Things that are too operational. Projects that are close to your heart and so you give in to the temptation to get into the weeds. Areas that you see as key and therefore feel you must lead on. After all, it's comfort zone territory and who doesn't feel comfortable in a comfort zone?

Of course to make sure that you are spending your time on the things that only you can do, letting go is crucial. And there is one essential element that supports this: making sure you have the right people in the right roles. Solve this problem and letting go suddenly becomes considerably easier. Elite athletes have an expert team alongside them: physio, strength and conditioning coach, nutritionist, coach. And this is just their sport team, before we even start listing their agents, lawyers and so on. They appoint them as the experts in their field, knowing that they can then trust them to do their job – meaning they can get on with theirs. You need to do the same.

Managing your energy

This is not about taking it easy or being 'soft'. It's about understanding that in order to perform at your best, over the long term, you have to look after body and mind. Why do athletes take this seriously? Because they know it's fundamental to performance. While you are not an elite athlete, you are a serious leader. Don't expect that you can deliver consistent, sustained performance without prioritizing the essential elements that go into your wellbeing: sleep and nutrition being at the top of the list. And Loehr's research (*see also* page 91) shows us the importance of focusing as well on the bite-sized gains. The busier you are, the more important it is to maintain your daily habits. The ones that have a really positive impact on your energy, your stamina and your state of mind. Stick to that 30-minute walk or workout every morning. Build in short micro breaks during the day. Allow yourself a short time to decompress at regular intervals. How can you maintain your effectiveness if you don't do this?

As Loehr's research shows us, it doesn't have to be a significant chunk of time. Even two minutes between meetings, if used correctly, can make a difference. This isn't just about a physical reset, it's also about a mental reset. The way in which Loehr's tennis players were using their mini-breaks meant that they could return to each point, and each game, with full focus. With 100 per cent intensity. Totally present for every point. Shouldn't you be aiming to do the same?

Try also to make sure that you are able to peak at the right times throughout the year. You can't be 'on' all the time. Whatever situation you are in, concentrate on making sure that you can ride the waves on a consistent basis. Maintaining the ebb and flow that's needed. Don't fight against it, go with it. Recognize the patterns, adapt your effort, maximize it when it's most needed and give yourself a breather when appropriate. Plan your rest and recovery blocks in an intentional and strategic way, recognizing that they are vital to long-term, sustained performance.

From the field of play to the corridors of leadership

Pervaze loved his last role. He was CEO of an organization of 50 people. He knew everyone well, he was on top of pretty much everything the organization was doing and enjoyed working alongside his colleagues on many of the projects they were involved with. In his new role, however, he has 650 people in the organization. His executive team, who all report into him, is made up of seven directors. He knows this is going to be a very different challenge and has asked for advice from one of his mentors, Ayesha.

Ayesha tells him that from her experience, the most important person in Pervaze's work life will be his executive assistant (EA). Not only does your EA help smooth your way, they also need to act as gatekeeper. But Ayesha stresses that to do this well, Pervaze has to give his EA good direction and clarity on what should come through to him (in terms of requests, diary appointments, etc.) and what should be re-directed elsewhere. Ayesha also highlights how important it will be for Pervaze to understand that he won't be able to operate as he did in his previous role. He won't be able to be across everything, and know everyone, in the business. His central internal relationships will be with his exec team. This is where he will need to focus his time and energy.

Ayesha noted that seven was quite a large number of direct reports and so suggested that when he starts the role, Pervaze examines this and reflects on whether this number could be reduced. And she stressed that alongside this, it was vital that Pervaze spend time at an early stage making sure he has the right people in those roles; people who he can really trust to fulfil their areas of responsibility in the best way possible.

Finally, Ayesha highlighted the fact that the bigger the organization, and the more responsibility on his shoulders, the greater the importance of focusing on, and prioritizing, his own energy levels and wellbeing. She recommended that Pervaze stick to simple, easy-to-achieve habits that ensure he maintains the right levels of health and stamina for his demanding role. Ayesha also recommended that Pervaze map out the next year in terms of Board meetings and reporting schedules, and mark in red the weeks of the year that he believes will be the ones that require maximum effort from him. Doing this will serve as a reminder to ensure his energy and stamina levels are at their highest for these periods. And finally, she reminded him of the importance of taking proper holidays, stressing that this was crucial for strong performance over the long term.

In summary

- Get clear on what your role involves. And what it does not involve.
- Use prompts and rules to keep to this.
- Develop your 'saying no' muscle.
- Use your support team to help you with this.
- Learn to let go – this is made easier by ensuring you have the right people in the right roles.
- Manage your energy – if you don't do this, you won't be able to perform and achieve over the long term.
- Alongside the significant aspects of sleep and nutrition, realize and harness the power of regular, short breaks during the working day.
- Build and maintain simple habits that are doable for you.
- Be aware of, and manage your energy around, the patterns and rhythms of your organization.
- Take proper rest and recovery blocks.
- Remember your growth mindset from Chapter 1 (*see also* pages 20–30) – this underpins everything.

PART TWO

Getting the Best Out of Those You Lead

'You don't build a business, you build people. And then people build the business.'

Henry Hilary 'Zig' Ziglar, American author and speaker

In sport, a coach's job is very simple – developing and improving their athletes. Every single day, the best coaches ask themselves: 'How can I help my athletes get better?'

This basic question should be the one sitting at the forefront of every leader's mind. In today's world, getting the best out of your people on a sustained basis will be what gives you a competitive advantage. What enables you to attract the best, retain the best and elicit the best performance over the long term? This is what will make the difference and this is what has been largely overlooked with all the focus on high performance and short-term winning.

Sport shows us that the same group of people can perform very differently when certain conditions are in place. Taking this insight from sport, overlaying it with research and insight from the world of work more generally, a pattern clearly emerges around the factors that make the difference. Connect this with the reality for many senior leaders on the ground and it becomes clear that these lessons from sport are game-changing, relevant and actionable.

In Part Two, we shine a spotlight on these factors that drive long-term performance from your people and explore how you can apply them to your daily and organizational working life with simple, practical and tangible steps.

CHAPTER SEVEN

How to Build Trust

'Money is the currency of transactions, but trust is the currency of interactions.'

Professor Rachel Botsman, author and trust expert

In the autumn of 2013, Jane Figueiredo was a hunted woman. A National Collegiate Athletic Association (NCAA) coaching legend, she had been head diving coach at the University of Houston for a number of years. Her 24-year tenure at the University had included 12 consecutive conference Diving Coach of the Year honours and four NCAA Diving Coach of the Year awards. Her divers had won multiple NCAA championships at Houston, in total eight NCAA titles and 51 All-American honours in 24 seasons.[59] She had also coached two Russian divers, Vera Ilyina and Yulia Pakhalina, to synchro springboard Gold at the 2000 Sydney Olympics.

In the autumn of 2013, someone wanted her services. And they were not prepared to take no for an answer. That someone was British diver Tom Daley. At 14, Daley had shot to fame, making the final of his event, the 10-metre platform, at the Beijing Olympics in 2008. Daley became World Champion at the event in 2009, when he was still only 15. He won Bronze at London 2012. But he was desperate to

---

[59] https://swimswam.com/houstons-jane-figueiredo-coach-tom-daley-londons-new-hp-diving-center/

fulfil his early potential and win Gold – and he believed Figueiredo was the coach to help him achieve this.

In October 2013, Figueiredo received a phone call. It was Daley, telling her that he was in Orlando, and was coming over to see her the next day. A bit taken aback, Figueiredo asked where he was going to be staying. 'With you,' he said. Come he did, and he stayed for two weeks. Figueiredo had been in Texas for nearly 30 years. It was warm, she liked it. Persuading her to move was going to be a hard job. Daley ended up visiting for a second time and again, Figueiredo's answer was 'No chance!' Eventually however, Daley convinced her and Figueiredo agreed to move to London at the beginning of 2014 to take over the new high-performance diving centre in the city, to where on the same day Daley moved his diving base.

Recently, Figueiredo was interviewed by Vicky Huyton, Founder of the Female Coaching Network.[60] In the interview, Huyton asked Figueiredo about her relationship with Daley and her other divers. In doing so, Huyton noted that throughout their conversation, what shone through was how much Figueiredo cared about her athletes – really cared about them. Figueiredo emphasized how important this was; noting the fact that you care gives you a licence to push and challenge more than if your athlete doesn't feel the love.

So, did Daley win that elusive Gold? Indeed he did. He and his partner, Matty Lee, completed a near-perfect final dive in the final round to win Gold in the men's synchronized 10-metre platform event at Tokyo 2020. And if you want to watch something short on YouTube that will bring a smile to your face, track down the video of Figueiredo literally jumping for joy and then into Daley's embrace, when the final scores were announced.

---

[60] https://femalecoachingnetwork.com/

Trust is so important in a coach-athlete relationship and on listening to Huyton questioning Figueiredo, it seemed to get to the core of the issue. In sport we often hear the expression 'the coach has lost the dressing room'. By this, the speaker/writer usually means that they are no longer trusted. The athletes no longer believe that the coach is going to get the best out of them, as individuals or as a team. And where that happens, the coach is, in colloquial terms, toast! Because to get the best out of others on a long-term basis, you have to push and challenge people. And if those people don't believe that you're someone who can help them towards their own goals and dreams, you will not be able to encourage and elicit the right levels of performance, growth and development.

It's equally important in leadership. In these uncertain times, when it's so much harder for people to feel their way, building trust within your teams and organizations is more important than ever. Certainly, if you want to get the best out of your people over the long term and enable them to achieve more than they thought possible. It's been posited that trust will be leadership's leading indicator in the 'next normal'[61] and Adam Grant, writing in the middle of the COVID-19 pandemic in *The Economist*[62], suggested that the level of trust we feel towards our colleagues and organizations is likely to become more extreme – in both directions.

If you want to get the best out of your people, on a consistent and sustained basis, trust is key.

How Do We Get This Wrong?

Let's look first at how this can go wrong in sport.

---

[61] https://www .mckinsey .com/~/media/mckinsey/email/leadingoff/2021/06/14/2021-06 -14b.html

[62] https://www.economist.com/by-invitation/2020/06/01/adam-grant-on-how-jobs-boss-es-and-firms-may-improve-after-the-crisis

Whose best interests?

Towards each and every elite athlete, their coach is in a position of huge responsibility; they effectively have their career in their hands. The custodian of the athlete's talent, their job is to enable them to fulfil their true potential. Trust is key. The athlete needs to believe that the coach is the right person to guide and challenge them, especially as their career (in relative terms) will only be short. If they don't trust their coach, if they don't believe the coach has their best long-term interests at heart, the relationship is not going to get the best out of them.

Let's use the example of an ambitious young coach who has just moved up to coach at a higher level of their particular sport. They've had a successful career to date, with their previous team being promoted three seasons in a row. The coach's aim is to coach a team in the top league. This new team is still two leagues away from this. Soon after starting, the coach begins to doubt the team's ability to make it to the top league; he feels it's just not going to be realistic for this team to get the right promotions. So, the coach's mindset changes; from focusing on where he can get this team to, to using this role as a platform to gain a job with a better team.

The players soon begin to pick up on this. How? Well, the coach's behaviour changes. It's not consistent with what it was. He no longer seems to want to really get to know the players as individuals; he doesn't seem prepared to put the time and effort in. The coach starts to make decisions and use language that suggests a focus on short-term wins rather than putting in the time and effort to build long-term success at the club. The previous coach at the club was very good at constantly reiterating and reinforcing the long-term vision for the club, something this new coach appeared to pay lip service to at the beginning and has now stopped referring to completely. And this new coach seems to be more bothered about his own career and prospects than those of his players.

Lack of expertise

What about the situation where a coach moves from one sport to another? There are quite a few examples of where this has gone wrong in elite sport. Often this comes down to a lack of faith in the coach's competence to deliver results in this new sport. Players will doubt the coach's understanding of the game: its nuances, patterns, history, context and so on. That's not to say that it can't work – there are some success stories in sport. But where it hasn't worked, the pattern around competence, and lack of faith in it, has been strong. As have issues around these coaches believing that they know it all already, they are expert coaches, and this belief restricting their willingness to really listen and learn.

Then again, where athletes do not trust their coach, the coach is not going to be able to push and challenge their athletes in a way that a more trusted coach could. And without this licence, they will not be able to get the best out of their athletes over the long term. Athletes will start to take shortcuts, commit less, skip sessions. And what happens then in a world that is generally performed at such a professional level? Standards drop, players stop developing and improving, and results go against the team.

Inconsistent behaviour

There is a belief within some areas of sport that it's good to keep your players on their toes, to keep them guessing, and that one way to achieve this is through inconsistent behaviour. Gentle and encouraging one day, tough and overly robust the next day. Talk to most athletes though and what they really value is consistency. Consistency in approach. Consistency in behaviour. Consistency in what the coaches value and what they don't. Consistency in the behaviours they support and those that they come down hard on.

While athletes will accept that there is a place for the occasional departure in approach, particularly when a coach needs to get a really significant point across, in general terms they are more able to trust their coaches when they know what to expect. Their focus needs to be on their improvement, on their development, not on what mood their coach is likely to be in that day.

Showing that you care

At the beginning of the chapter we looked at how central caring about your people is to trust and there is a salutary tale from the world of hockey that demonstrates that it's not just enough to care, you have to actually make sure your people truly believe this. We first came across Danny Kerry in Chapter 3 (*see also* page 51). Kerry is a coach who has been involved in elite hockey in England and Great Britain for a long time. He has had great success and is an exceptional coach. Like everyone though, he did not come fully formed and has had some hard lessons to learn along the way. Some of these came after the 2008 Olympics in Beijing. He'd been appointed as head coach to the GB Women's squad in 2007 and led them to sixth place at the Olympics the following year. At the same time GB was seeded below this in the world and he felt he had done a pretty good job.

The post-Olympics 360 review suggested otherwise. In fact, some of the feedback on Kerry was brutal. One thing in particular that was highlighted by the players was the extent to which he genuinely cared about his players as people. Not enough was the answer. As Kerry has shared publicly many times, he did care. A lot. He just wasn't very good at showing it. One of the reasons I have highlighted Danny Kerry is that his story is such a brilliant example of the growth mindset underpinning this whole book. Despite the incredibly harsh feedback that Kerry received back in 2008 (or more accurately, because of it), he took it on board, knuckled down and worked extremely hard at building and developing his abilities in the areas where he had historically fallen short.

It's not just in sport that trust is key. The same applies in other high-performance environments. Simon Sinek has shared in his book *The Infinite Game*[63] the surprising approach that the Navy SEALs take to trust versus performance. The US Navy sea air and land teams, SEALs for short, are the US Navy's primary special operations force. Selection is fierce and they are tasked with the most high-pressure missions there are. To determine the kind of person who belongs in the SEALs, one of the things they do is to evaluate candidates on two axes: performance versus trust. As Sinek explains, performance is about technical competence. How good someone is at their job. Do they have grit? Can they remain cool under pressure? Trust is about character. Their humility and sense of personal accountability. How much they have their teammates' back and whether they are a positive influence on team members. In an ideal world, everyone would be in the top-right corner of the graph: high performance and high trust. The SEALs discovered that the top-left corner is not good, the high performer of low trust is a toxic team member. These team members exhibit traits of narcissism, are quick to blame others, put themselves first. And what's really surprising is that the SEALs would rather have a medium performer of high trust, sometimes even a low performer of high trust, than a high performer of low trust.[64]

Where does vulnerability fit in?

The link between vulnerability and trust has been widely made in recent times, with the ability to share or demonstrate vulnerability a topic that has been explored extensively by authors such as Simon

[63] Simon Sinek, *The Infinite Game*, Penguin Business, 2019.
[64] Simon Sinek, *The Infinite Game*, Penguin Business, 2019, pp. 109–110.

Sinek, Brené Brown and Daniel Coyle. At face value, it's easy to assume from some of the commentary in this area that showing vulnerability builds trust. Period. However, as these and other authors and commentators have already highlighted, there are nuances to this. Being vulnerable, feeling vulnerable and demonstrating and sharing this does have its place in building trust among those you lead. There needs though to be boundaries to this.

Imagine a coach starting a new role. In their first meeting with their squad, they decide to share their vulnerability, believing, after a quick read of some leadership material over the summer break, that this will help build trust among their players. The coach talks about how this is their first role at this level. How they have imposter syndrome. How they expect to make a huge number of mistakes. What do you think the impact will be on the squad? What will the players be muttering to each other as they leave that first meeting?

There is a time and a place for vulnerability, but it has to be well-framed and well-timed. As Brené Brown herself said in a recent podcast with Simon Sinek, vulnerability needs boundaries. Brown shared a story of delivering some training to a group of new CEOs in Silicon Valley – she had been brought in by the investors. Part of her talk was about vulnerability, and as she finished, one of the CEOs came running up to her and basically said, 'That was amazing, I'm going to go back to my employees and investors and let them know that I'm in over my head, we are bleeding money and I don't know what to do.' Brown recounts in the podcast how she gently suggested to the CEO that he had missed the part of her talk where she talked about vulnerability with boundaries, asking why he would share this with a bunch of people who had followed this CEO into the company and put their career in his hands.[65] (NB: Brown also made

---

[65] https://www.youtube.com/watch?v=J16Zyknu9Mw

the point that she hoped that the individual would be sharing this with someone, rather than not at all, that someone hopefully being a mentor or a coach.)

Trust is key. And as with coaching, so with leadership.

If your people don't believe that you have their best interests at heart, that you are only in it for yourself, that you don't believe in them, that you don't really care, that you are not in fact capable, they are not going to trust in your leadership. And so you will lose the dressing room. You will not have the licence you need to challenge your team, push them, direct their energies towards the long-term success of the business. They will not be willing to exert themselves to the full, to really take the brakes off. Instead, they will disengage, reduce their commitment, reduce their energy. You might be able to solve this problem in the short term with sticking plasters such as more money, but you won't be able to get the best out of them over the long term.

So, what is it that you need to do? How can you build the trust needed to get the best out of your people over the long term?

Getting the Best Out of Your People – On a Sustained Basis

Demonstrate that you are capable

The people you lead need to see that you are capable. That doesn't mean that you have all the answers. And it certainly doesn't mean that you are perfect. It does mean though that you have sufficient ability, experience, skillset, mindset and adaptability to lead your team and/or organization through the challenges and opportunities ahead. And that you are capable enough to know where you need to develop and improve, and are able to go about doing so.

So, how can you ensure, and demonstrate, this? First, be clear on what you bring to the table. Don't hide your light under a bushel.

There is never a need to brag and certainly don't oversell, however remember the impact of calmly instilling in those around you confidence that your experience, expertise and mindset set you up well for your role. Second, be honest about your gaps and areas of weakness and ensure that you work out a way to fill them. This is where the vulnerability element comes into positive effect. No one expects you to be a robot or to have everything covered. And it's OK to be comfortable with this and share this, but they do need to know that you have a plan to plug the gaps.

Demonstrate that you care

For me, this is a simple way of articulating some of the key aspects within trust that are written about extensively. Empathy. Integrity. Accountability. Responsibility. Vulnerability. Compassion. If you care about the organization's purpose, care about the organization itself and care about your people, all of these attributes should flow. And it should be clear to your people that you are coming at it from the right place.

Work hard to look under the bonnet and understand issues being faced, both at an organizational and at a personal level. Walk the corridors. Talk to people. In sport, the best coaches follow the maxim 'Person Before Player'. How hard have you worked at getting to know your people, at least those with whom you work on a daily basis?

Focus on being informed and accessible with good processes in place to ensure this.

Communicate. Regularly and openly. And repeat, consistently, the purpose and vision so everyone around you is reminded that these are your guiding lights, not your own self-interest.

'People don't care how much you know until they know how much you care.'

Theodore Roosevelt, US President

Be consistent

If you behave in a way that is consistent, that people around you can rely on, if you walk the talk, and honour your commitments, you engender confidence in those around you. And that's key to gaining their trust. Think about it for a moment. Think about those leaders who don't operate in this way. Who are unpredictable. Who don't do what they say they are going to do. Who expect one thing and do another. Who one day behave in a certain way and another day entirely differently. Unhelpful. The opposite of reassuring. And frankly, the last thing we need in an increasingly uncertain and volatile world.

Remember that as a leader you are constantly role-modelling the values and behaviours you want to see. You are also role-modelling what you are willing, and unwilling, to accept: 'The standard you walk past is the standard you become'. This was a mantra used to great effect by Ben Ryan, who coached Fiji's Rugby Sevens team to their country's first ever Olympic Gold at the Rio Olympics in 2016. Ryan is a fabulous example of someone who really cared about his players and had a forensic focus on behaviours and standards, all documented in his book, *Sevens Heaven*[66].

Honour your commitments and keep your promises. And if for any (genuinely good) reason you can't, communicate this in good time and explain why. While being aware that you need to adapt at times, and should also be seeking to continuously improve, don't try and be something you're not.

---

[66] Ben Ryan, *Sevens Heaven: The Beautiful Chaos of Fiji's Olympic Dream*, Weidenfeld & Nicolson, 2019.

The Three Core Elements

The Three Core Elements

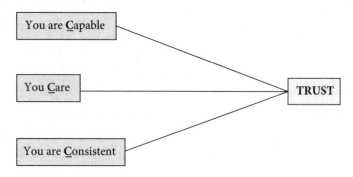

From the field of play to the corridors of leadership

Lucie has recently taken on her first headship. It's a significant step for her and one about which she is both excited and slightly daunted. The role is in a school where Lucie has not worked before and she realizes that one of the first things she has to accomplish is to ensure that the staff and parents believe in her; that they trust that she is the right person to lead the school. This is particularly important for Lucie, as she has come into the role with a remit from the Board of Governors to drive change. The school's performance has dipped in recent years and Lucie has a hard job in front of her to bring the school back up to the level of performance that the governors know it can achieve.

Lucie has already set out her vision and proposed strategy as part of the interview process. In her first session with the whole staff team, she shares this with them, reinforcing throughout her speech the high standards and performance that she is aiming to move the school towards. She is very clear in her own mind that, alongside this, she needs to use this opportunity to demonstrate to her staff why she is the right person for the role; what it is about her background, her experience and her skillset that will enable her to lead the school in its turnaround. She balances this with an acknowledgement that she doesn't have all the answers and that this is of course her first headship. She will need the support and wisdom of her colleagues if they are really going to build and improve the school in the way that's needed.

In addition to this whole staff session, Lucie sets herself the target of speaking to all staff members individually within the first six weeks of her tenure. She uses these opportunities to get to know them as individuals, listen to their perspectives and thoughts on the school and reinforce her own messaging around the new vision for the school, her determination to achieve it and the hard work and standards that will be required to reach it.

In summary

- In order to get sustained, long-term performance, you have to push and challenge your people.
- This requires that your people trust you; that you are the right person to be leading them.
- They need to see that you are capable, that you have the ability and skill to lead them.
- You need to show them that you care.
- And you need to be consistent in your behaviours.
- Vulnerability has its place, but it needs boundaries.
- Remember your growth mindset from Chapter 1 (*see also* pages 20–30) – this underpins everything.

CHAPTER EIGHT

How to Instil the Right Balance of Belief

'Champions keep playing until they get it right.'

Billie Jean King, American tennis player

June 1987 and a basketball coach was about to make a prophecy that few coaches would dare to make …

The Los Angeles Lakers had just won the NBA Championship. Amid the champagne corks popping and the noise and hubbub of celebration, head coach Pat Riley was approached by a reporter. This reporter had just one question on his mind: could the Lakers be the first team in almost 20 years to win the NBA championship twice in a row? 'Can you repeat?' the reporter asked Riley. Quick as a flash, Riley replied: 'I guarantee it.' The reporter was taken aback, he had to make sure he had heard right. 'Guarantee?' he asked. 'That's right,' said Riley.

I first came across this story in Tali Sharot's book *The Optimism Bias: Why We're Wired to Look on the Bright Side*[67]. In the book, Sharot emphasizes that Riley's guarantee, delivered not just to the journalists but to the players and millions of fans, was not a one-off celebration induced piece of madness. Riley repeated the guarantee during the team's victory parade in downtown LA and continued to

---

[67] Tali Sharot, *The Optimism Bias: Why We're Wired to Look on the Bright Side*, Robinson 2012.

do so again and again throughout the summer and into the 1987–88 season.

So, what happened? Did he end up looking a genius or just the opposite?

One year after Riley's guarantee, the Los Angeles Lakers were once more in the NBA finals. This time their opponents were the Detroit Pistons, known for being tough and hungry. The battle was tight, the lead constantly swinging from one team to the other. With six seconds to go, the Lakers were ahead by one point, 106 to 105. During those six seconds, they managed to score once more and won the last game 108–105, making good on Riley's guarantee.

Straight after, Riley was once again in front of the cameras. 'Can you do it again?' the reporters asked. 'Will there be a threepeat?' We'll never know what Riley was going to answer as before any words could leave his mouth, one of his players, Kareem Abdul-Jabbar, covered Riley's lips with his hands just in time to prevent the coach from speaking. Riley never guaranteed the threepeat; despite this, the Lakers again found themselves in the NBA finals, once more versus the Detroit Pistons. This time the Pistons won the series. As Sharot asks, would the Lakers have won a third consecutive championship if Riley had promised it? We will never know.[68]

When I read this story a few years back, it set my mind racing. About optimism. About belief. About the balance between these and reality. I had recently seen an article on Jonathan Edwards, a triple jumper who was the first man on earth to jump more than 60ft. An Olympic and World Champion triple jumper, he was also a devout Christian. Edwards has held the world record for the men's triple jump since 1995 and he has often talked about how his athletics career was sustained by his faith. Not just his career, but his incredible

---

[68] Tali Sharot, *The Optimism Bias: Why We're Wired to Look on the Bright Side*, Robinson, 2012, pp. 40–42.

performances. His belief was that he had an ability given to him by God and so it was his responsibility to make the most of it. This belief in God also helped him in those big moments of pressure, where he felt the result was almost out of his hands and more about God's will. While Edwards has since talked publicly about his subsequent loss of faith, and now describes himself as a devout atheist, there is no doubting the help he felt he had received by virtue of his faith at the time he was competing. Indeed, he has referred to it as sports psychology in all but name.

As with Edwards, so too three-times World Heavyweight boxing champion Muhammad Ali, who once famously said: 'How can I lose when I have Allah on my side?' And it's not just belief around something that is arguably intangible. Sport also shows us how powerful tangible belief can be. The story of how Roger Bannister broke the four-minute mile in May 1954 is well known. What's less well known is what happened shortly afterwards. Bannister's successful attempt was months in the planning. It was the result of a carefully targeted training regime and a forensic approach to the race on the day. And it was a goal that, according to a *Harvard Business Review* article published shortly after Bannister's death in 2018, runners had been trying to break since 1886.[69] It's easy to imagine that it took a while before anyone else was able to repeat the feat. In fact, this couldn't be further from the truth. Just 46 days after Bannister's feat, Australian runner John Landy broke the barrier again, with a time of 3 minutes 58 seconds. One year later, three runners broke the four-minute barrier *in a single race*. Over the last half century, more than 1,000 runners have conquered a barrier that had once been considered hopelessly out of reach.

---

[69] https://hbr.org/2018/03/what-breaking-the-4-minute-mile-taught-us-about-the-limits-of-conventional-thinking

As in sport, so too in leadership, which is about getting the best out of your people. And to do this in a sustainable way, in a way that drives consistent results, belief needs to play its part. The question is, what part, and how important is it to performance? In short, the answer is more than you might imagine. In fact, two Wharton School professors have analyzed the lessons for business of the four-minute mile. In their book, *The Power of Impossible Thinking*[70], Yoram Wind and Colin Cook devote an entire chapter to an assessment of Bannister's feat and emphasize the mindset behind it rather than the physical achievement. How is it, they wonder, that so many runners smashed the four-minute barrier after Bannister became the first to do it? 'Was there a sudden growth spurt in human evolution? Was there a genetic engineering experiment that created a new race of super runners? No. What changed was the mental model. The runners of the past had been held back by a mindset that said they could not surpass the four-minute mile. When that limit was broken, the others saw that they could do something they had previously thought impossible.'

How Do We Get This Wrong?

In my view there are two sins of belief: limiting belief and unjustified belief.

Limiting belief

David Robson, author of *The Intelligence Trap*, published in 2019[71], has more recently turned his attention to expectations and their impact on outcomes. The central argument in Robson's science-

---

[70] Yoram (Jerry) R. Wind and Colin Cook, *The Power of Impossible Thinking: Transform the Business of Your Life and the Life of Your Business,* Financial Times/Prentice Hall, 2006.
[71] David Robson, *The Intelligence Trap: Revolutionise Your Thinking and Make Wiser Decisions,* Hodder & Stoughton, 2019.

backed book, *The Expectation Effect* is that our brains are 'prediction machines', steering us through life by generating expectations and only revising them when unavoidable. These expectations play a vital role in shaping what we experience. He starts with the story of dozens of apparently healthy young men who had emigrated from Laos and were dying in their sleep in the late 1970s. The phenomenon was termed 'sudden unexpected nocturnal death syndrome'; really just a label to cover the epidemiologists' confusion and lack of understanding. As Robson writes, today, we think we know the cause: the men experienced sleep paralysis. While fairly common and harmless in itself, the men understood it as a visitation from the *dab tsog*, a malevolent spirit who sits on victims' chests at night. Across the world, far from the shamans and others who could have helped them to ward off the evil, the men panicked, probably exacerbating a form of heart arrhythmia more prevalent in people from Southeast Asia, and triggering the cardiac arrest.[72]

Robson goes on to demonstrate how if you believe that ageing is a matter of inevitable cognitive decline and reducing usefulness to society, you're more likely to experience hearing loss, frailty and even Alzheimer's. All of this inevitably brings to mind motor company founder Henry Ford's well-known saying: 'Whether you think you can or think you can't, you're right.'

As a leader, if you limit the beliefs of the people in your organization, you are falling foul of this sin of belief. And in doing so, you are not going to be able to get the best out of your people on a sustained basis over the long term. Sport shows us time and again that it's possible to achieve in situations and circumstances that seem beyond hope.

---

[72] David Robson, *The Expectation Effect: How Your Mindset Can Transform Your Life*, Canongate Books, 2022, pp. 2–3.

Unjustified belief

What about the other sin of belief, unjustified belief? Over-confident belief. Belief that is not backed up by any sense of feasibility or any sense of the work, strategy, focus and effort that needs to go into it becoming true.

Imagine if Pat Riley had given that guarantee of his team winning the double if he didn't have strong foundations in place to make it viable. To make it possible. He knew that the team understood what it would take to win the Championship – after all, they had just done so. He had the players; he had Magic Johnson, James Worthy and Kareem Abdul-Jabbar! He had the structure. He had the set-up. Guaranteeing it was a strong call. But it wasn't a baseless claim.

And we can turn to insight from Jim Collins, together with one of the most formidable military officers of all time, to reinforce this. We have come across Collins earlier on in this book, with his work *Good to Great: Why Some Companies Make the Leap…and Others Don't*[73] (*see also* page 22). As Collins writes, every good-to-great company faced significant adversity along the way to greatness, of one sort or another. In every case, the management team responded with a powerful psychological duality. On the one hand, they stoically accepted the brutal facts of reality. On the other, they maintained an unwavering faith in the endgame and a commitment to prevail as a great company despite the brutal facts.

Collins and his team came to call this duality the Stockdale Paradox.[74] The name refers to Admiral Jim Stockdale, who was the highest-ranking United States military officer in the 'Hanoi Hilton' prisoner-of-war camp during the height of the Vietnam War. Tortured

---

[73] Jim Collins, *Good to Great: Why Some Companies Make the Leap…and Others Don't*, New York, HarperCollins, 2001.

[74] https://www.jimcollins.com/concepts/Stockdale-Concept.html#:~:text=Every%20good%2Dto%2Dgreat%20company,reality%2C%20whatever%20they%20might%20be

over 20 times during his eight-year imprisonment from 1965 to 1973, Stockdale lived out the war without any prisoner's rights, no set release date and no certainty as to whether he would even survive to see his family again.

Collins tells the story of being invited by Stockdale to lunch. In preparation, he read *In Love and War*, the harrowing book written by Stockdale and his wife Sybil[75]. Collins was fascinated by how Stockdale had not just survived when so many hadn't, but had come out of it and flourished, so he put just this question to Stockdale while they were on a gentle walk before lunch. Stockdale responded by saying: 'I never lost faith in the end of the story, I never doubted not only that I would get out, but also that I would prevail in the end and turn the experience into the defining event of my life, which, in retrospect, I would not trade.'

After some time to take stock of this answer, Collins then asked, 'Who didn't make it out?'

'Oh, that's easy,' Stockdale said. 'The optimists.'

'The optimists? I don't understand,' said Collins, now completely confused, given what he'd said about 100 metres earlier.

'The optimists. Oh, they were the ones who said, "We're going to be out by Christmas." And Christmas would come, and Christmas would go. Then they'd say, "We're going to be out by Easter." And Easter would come, and Easter would go. And then Thanksgiving, and then it would be Christmas again. And they died of a broken heart.'

Another long pause, and more walking. Then Stockdale turned to Collins and said, 'This is a very important lesson. You must never confuse faith that you will prevail in the end – which you can never afford to lose – with the discipline to confront the most brutal facts of your current reality, whatever they might be.'

---

[75] Jim and Sibyl Stockdale, *In Love and War: The Story of a Family's Ordeal and Sacrifice during the Vietnam Years,* Naval Institute Press, 1990.

Sport does this second element particularly well. One of the benefits of competing against opponents is that it shows you where you are at the present time. It confronts you with the harsh reality. It ensures that alongside the belief that you will prevail, you have clarity on where you are now. And how much hard work is needed to get to where you want to get to. Competition provides an objective indication of, and reminder, that you are not yet where you need to be.

Outside of sport it can be harder to both understand and face this reality. Harder to get the opportunity. And perhaps more of a temptation to sugar-coat the message. So, how can you get this right as leader? How can you instil the right levels of belief in your people, both in terms of the organization and in terms of their own performance? Find this sweet spot of belief and not only will you reap the benefits in the short term, you are giving yourself a much better chance of getting the best out of your people on a sustained basis, over the long term. With belief acting as a constant anchor for everyone's effort, motivation and dedication.

Getting the Best Out of Your People – On a Sustained Basis

At the organization level

Purpose and vision

One of the things that always strikes me when working with organizations in the sports sector is how important purpose is to them. To share an example, while working with one organization to help define its future strategy, I asked each member of the Board to articulate what they believed the purpose of the organization was. Half an hour later I was floating on a tide of enthusiasm, passion and conviction. Each member, while articulating the purpose in a slightly different way, was clear and resolute about the positive impact their organization had on the health and happiness of so many people.

The argument that having a clear purpose can drive sustained performance is increasingly being backed up by evidence. Doing so establishes why an organization exists and what problems it is here to solve. A 2020 Deloitte Insights Paper, titled 'Purpose is Everything', started by stating that purpose-driven companies witness higher market share gains and grow three times faster on average than their competitors, all while achieving higher workforce and customer satisfaction.[76]

For many organizations, a clear vision will sit alongside their purpose, one that is authentically held and demonstrated, and that acts as the organization's North Star. Setting out what their people need to be striving towards. Good purpose and vision statements are positive, aspirational and motivating. Rather than short-term goals, they are long-term dreams that inspire action. If your people truly believe in the organization's purpose and vision, truly get behind it, you will unleash their potential in a much more effective way for the long term. (An important point to note: don't get too hung up on terminology. What is one company's vision is often another company's mission or purpose. Generally, purpose is centred on why you exist and vision is centred on your picture of the future.)

Unfortunately, even for those organizations who have poured often huge amounts of money and resource into the development and articulation of an organization's purpose and vision, many organizations are let down by a singular failure; the unwillingness, inability or hesitancy of leadership to consistently make sure that they are front and centre. In this regard I believe that leaders need to sound like a broken record, constantly reinforcing their organization's purpose and vision. Why it exists. What it is trying to achieve. This should be articulated at every opportunity you have, whether internal

---

[76] https://www2.deloitte.com/us/en/insights/topics/marketing-and-sales-operations/global-marketing-trends/2020/purpose-driven-companies.html

or external. Building and leveraging the belief that achieving it is indeed possible.

We have already referenced Simon Sinek and his latest book, *The Infinite Game*. In his book, he posits that the title CEO should be replaced with the title CVO: Chief Vision Officer. How many times each week do you as a leader articulate your organization's purpose and vision? Once? Twice? It should be every single day. And when you do so, do you do it with conviction? As if you truly believe it? Or in a half-hearted way, a way that is meant to demonstrate to the listener that you are a bit uncomfortable saying it? If you don't believe it, why should your people?

Growth mindset

We examined growth mindset for you as leader in Chapter 1 of this book (*see also* pages 20–30). Many of you reading that chapter will have realized the relevance of growth mindset more broadly across your organization.

Satya Nadella formed just this connection when he made growth mindset one of the central planks of his new regime at Microsoft. Back in 2014, Nadella was appointed as only the third-ever CEO of Microsoft. He came in at a time when the company was going backwards and had huge numbers of problems to deal with. He knew that things had to change. Out of work, Nadella had a child with special needs and because of this he spent a lot of time perusing research in the education world. One day he came across Carol Dweck (who we met in Chapter 1) and the work she was doing around growth mindset. The more he read, the more he realized this was what is needed at Microsoft in order to drive improved and sustained performance.[77]

---

[77] Satya Nadella, *Hit Refresh: The Quest to Rediscover Microsoft's Soul and Imagine a Better Future for Everyone*, William Collins, 2018.

Why is growth mindset important at the organization level? Because it feeds into the second aspect of the Stockdale Paradox (*see also* page 123). The understanding and realization that working towards the organization's purpose is not going to be easy. Progress won't be linear. Huge amounts of well-targeted effort will be required. Initiatives will need to be trialled, with no guarantee that everything will work. People will need to be comfortable with the uncomfortable. The culture will need to support innovation, bounded risk-taking and a rapid learning from both success and failure. All underpinned by a central understanding that achieving the aspirational is possible, only with tremendous effort from all.

At the individual level

How do you engender the right level of belief in your people at an individual level? Again, supporting the development of a growth mindset within each person is going to be critical. What you do at the organization-wide level can either enhance or reduce your chances of doing this successfully, as can every coaching conversation that takes place with the organization. We'll turn to some seventh-grade students in the States to demonstrate this, in a study I first read about in Dan and Chip Heath's book, *The Power of Moments*.

Psychologist David Scott Yeager and eight colleagues ran a study in a suburban junior high school in which 44 seventh-grade students were assigned to write an essay about a personal hero. Their teachers then marked up the essays, providing written feedback. At that point, the researchers collected the papers from the teachers and split the essays randomly into two piles. They appended a generic note, in the teacher's handwriting, to each essay in the first pile. It said, 'I'm giving you these comments so that you'll have feedback on your paper.' The essays in the second pile got a note reflecting what the researchers call 'wise criticism'. It said: 'I'm giving you these comments because I have very high expectations and I know you can reach them.' (High standards and assurance.)

After the papers were returned, the students had the option to revise and resubmit their paper in the hopes of earning a better grade. About 40 per cent of the students who got the generic note chose to revise their papers. Almost 80 per cent of the wise criticism students revised their papers and in editing their papers, they made more than twice as many corrections as the other students.

As I have said, I first heard about this research from Dan and Chip Heath's book *The Power of Moments* (we have come across them before with their book, *Switch*[78]). In their reflections on this story, they consider what makes the second note so powerful. It rewires the way students process criticism. The wise criticism note carries a message that says: 'I know you're capable of great things if you'll just put in the work. The marked-up essay is not a personal judgement. It's a push to stretch.'[79]

This story reinforces the importance of finding that sweet spot of belief. Let your people know that you believe in them. That you have high expectations and know they can achieve them. Equally, help them confront the reality in front of them. Let them know that in order to do so, they are going to have to develop, grow and work hard. If they believe they can, and you help them to do so, you will enable them to perform and achieve over the long term.

There are countless examples in sport of coaches who use this approach. Who go out of their way to reinforce (privately and often publicly) how much they believe in particular players, how high their expectations are. But make sure that they balance this with a focus on the hard work they need to put in to achieve this. Coaches do this

---

[78] Chip and Dan Heath, *Switch: How to Change Things When Change is Hard*, Random House Business Books, 2011.

[79] Dan and Chip Heath, *The Power of Moments*, Bantam Press, 2017, pp. 122–3.

because they know the first helps the second. By making it clear that they truly believe in their players, they are helping and encouraging them to push and stretch themselves to improve and develop – and so achieve over the long term.

But we haven't covered the whole story of the High Standards + Assurance framework. We will revisit it in Chapter 11 and discover how to adapt it to truly develop your people in a long-term way.

From the field of play to the corridors of leadership

Dan had been CEO of his organization for the last three years. The business had been struggling when he took the role and one of his first priorities was to repurpose it. The existing Purpose and Vision Statement was no longer appropriate or effective so he commissioned a project that re-set what the company was all about. This six-month project led to a new Purpose and Vision Statement: one that was aspirational, inclusive and positive. Buy-in from the organization was good due to the inclusive process that had been followed.

Dan was clear that this was only the first stage of the process. He constantly emphasized to his leadership team that the hard work was still to come: properly embedding the Purpose and Vision and consistently reinforcing it; every internal document, right down to meeting agendas and project reports, had the Purpose and Vision statement on them. He opened every single leadership team meeting with the statement and asked that each team manager do the same. He also made sure that at every Leadership Team Away Day, which took place each quarter, the team reviewed their progress towards their Purpose and Vision, took honest stock of where they were and used this analysis in the continued development of their strategy and operational plans.

One of Dan's first appointments when he joined the organization was a new HR manager, whom he knew from his previous organization. He appointed him because of his success there in embedding a growth mindset culture and tasked him to do the same at this company. Both men understood that this would take time and require work and changes across the organization, encompassing structure and processes as well as the all-important work on values and behaviours. They knew how important this was in getting the best out of their people in a sustainable way.

(We will look in more detail at the mechanics of embedding a growth mindset culture in Chapter 11.)

In summary

- Beware the two sins of belief: limiting beliefs and unjustified beliefs.
- Aim for the Stockdale Paradox – faith that you will prevail, balanced with the discipline to confront reality. This is relevant at the organization level, as well as the individual level.
- Use your organization's purpose and vision to reinforce what your organization is working towards and drive belief in the ability of the organization to do so.
- Consistently articulate and reinforce it – with conviction.
- Underpin this with an environment and culture that supports a growth mindset.
- Let your people know that you believe in them and that they need to continually grow and develop in order to achieve.

CHAPTER NINE

How to Foster Belonging

'It's not the winning. It's how you win. The people you win with, the group of people you are connected to. I think that human connection is the ultimate marker of success.'

Alex Danson, GB hockey player

It's Game Day. A home game at the beginning of the season. And the team want to get off to the best start possible. The players arrive in good time and go through their pre-set routines and warm-ups. The match starts. Four 15-minute quarters. It's fast and furious, with the lead changing throughout. In the final minute, the home team scores to take the lead. Match won. Celebrations all round. The players warm down, debrief and go home.

Or do they?

The sport is netball. And the team is London Pulse.

UK's netball super league (now called the Vitality Super League) was founded in 2005. It's the UK's top-level, elite netball competition, now featuring 10 teams from England, Wales and Scotland. In 2017, three new franchises made their debuts: Severn Stars, Scottish Sirens and Wasps. The announcement of the Severn Stars franchise particularly caught my interest; the franchise was established as a joint venture between the University of Worcester and the University of Gloucestershire. I grew up just outside of Gloucester. At the time the new franchise was announced, I remember feeling quite surprised. Growing up, representing my county of Gloucestershire in various sports, Worcestershire were our rivals. Now they were being put together in a franchise that required them to belong together?

It led me to contemplate the nature of belonging in sport: why it mattered and what factors went into ensuring it. And led me to a conversation on this topic with Sam Bird. Bird came in as assistant coach of the Severn Stars when the franchise was set up, moving up to head coach on the resignation of Mo'onia Gerrard in 2017. She worked in that role for three years before being appointed as CEO and director of netball at another of the Vitality Super League franchises, London Pulse. Like me, Bird worked as a solicitor for many years. She had also played netball for England and maintained her connection with the sport throughout her legal career, before making the move across to a full-time sports role.

Talking to Bird, what immediately became clear was both the challenges faced by a franchise like London Pulse and her understanding of what really matters. In that story above, the players didn't all go home after their debrief – they stayed together for a post-match meal. Bird insisted on this because for her, Game Day doesn't just involve the sport. Game Day also involves the vital bonding time together as a team. Bird asserts strongly that the last bit of Game Day, the post-match meal, is just as important to becoming a championship team as all the other elements of the day. The two hours spent over food and drink are a vital element in making a sustainable championship team, impacting on good recruitment, player retention and on-court performance. Because this is where deeper relationships are formed, genuine conversations happen, players and coaches can really get to understand each other as people. Where people can feel like they truly belong. And where the identity that the franchise is aiming to build and embed can be reinforced at a deeper level.

Belonging is important to leadership outside of sport. People like to belong, it's a basic human need. As Owen Eastwood says in his book *Belonging: The Ancient Code of Togetherness*, Homo Sapiens' evolutionary story unequivocally tells us that the purpose of groups is to promote the wellbeing of their people.[80]

A 2021 McKinsey & Company study asked employers why they thought their employees had recently quit. The employers believed it was because of compensation, work-life balance and poor physical and emotional health. And were they right? Yes, these issues did matter to employees. However, not as much as employers thought they did. For a whopping 51 per cent of employees, it was because they didn't feel a sense of belonging at work.[81]

By not understanding what their people are running from or being drawn towards, leaders are not going to get the best out of them on a consistent basis; they are not going to be able to drive sustained effort and performance. And the move towards hybrid working (the flexible model where employees work partly in the workplace, and partly remotely) promotes a strange tension: a need to devote even more resources to ensuring a sense of belonging, while making it significantly harder to do so, particularly if you expect simply to deploy the same old initiatives.

How Do We Get This Wrong?

Lack of clear identity

London Pulse is the most diverse of all the Super League franchises. Over 30 languages are spoken throughout the club and the players are incredibly socially and ethnically diverse, ranging from Oxbridge law graduates to athletes living in houses where meeting the cost of living

[80] Owen Eastwood, *Belonging: The Ancient Code of Togetherness*, Quercus Editions Ltd, 2021, p. 132.
[81] https://www.mckinsey.com/business-functions/people-and-organizational-performance/our-insights/great-attrition-or -great-attraction-the-choice-is-yours

is a challenge. Sam Bird was clear in our conversation that creating a strong sense of identity around the franchise, to align this diverse set of athletes behind something relevant and compelling, is critical to success. Netball is a possession game and 'London Pulse Wins Ball' is an integral part of their identity as is their off-court ideology of being humble. This concept is interwoven with everything the club does, whether it's how they interact with the community they are in or who they reach out to. They are the first netball club in the world to offer free netball programmes for visually impaired athletes. Their 'being humble' mantra sits behind the franchise's broader purpose, which is to enhance young women's lives in and around London. This has led the club to support a scheme run by the Metropolitan Police that aims to draw women away from crime, with players from the franchise volunteering on the programme to coach and inspire. All of this aimed towards establishing a clear identity for an incredibly and brilliantly diverse organization.

As Howard Schultz, founder of Starbucks, famously said: 'People want to be part of something larger than themselves. They want to be part of something they are really proud of, that they'll fight for, sacrifice for, that they trust.'

Elite sports teams work hard on this element. Coaching staff know the positive impact it can have. It's why the England men's football set up has a new ritual: that of awarding legacy caps to debutants to the team. From September 2021, all debutants are awarded a special red velvet cap with their newly established legacy number embroidered on the front.[82] Just one of the initiatives aimed at increasing that powerful sense of belonging that the squad put into practice, as a result of the work done with Owen Eastwood.

---

[82] https://www.englandfootball.com/articles/2021/Jun/08/20210608-england-legacy-caps -awarded-to-squad-members

Fitting in versus belonging

In his book *Belonging*, Owen Eastwood shares the story of Michael Owen, an English football player. Michael Owen made his debut in the England team aged just 18 years and one month, the youngest player to do so at that time. He had grown up through the youth system at Liverpool football club, making his senior debut there at just 17, and went on to play for Liverpool for eight years, scoring 158 goals in 297 games. Eastwood describes Owen's strong sense of belonging at Liverpool, with Owen explaining that everyone knew him as a person, not just a player. An environment which felt safe, where he could relax and get on with the job.

In 2004, Owen transferred to Real Madrid CF. The team there, known as the 'Galácticos', included a host of world-class players including Zinedine Zidane, Raúl, Luís Figo, (Brazilian) Ronaldo and David Beckham. Owen never fully settled at the club, returning to England at the end of a single season which was, for him personally, a disappointing one. In discussing this with Eastwood, he highlighted his need and desire to feel accepted by the other players; the hope that his style of play would fit; how the fans would take to him. None of which he had even considered when he was at Liverpool. As he shared with Eastwood: 'I felt I belonged from a talent point of view, but I felt less confident in the social space of the team. I struggled to assert my personality and allow them to get to know me as a person. I went from a prankster in the Liverpool dressing room to feeling a little like an outsider.'[83]

We have already highlighted the work that Professor Brené Brown (lecturer, author and podcast host) has done around vulnerability. She has also talked extensively about the contrast between fitting

---

[83] Owen Eastwood, *Belonging: The Ancient Code of Togetherness*, Quercus Editions Ltd, 2021, pp. 32–33.

in and belonging. In a popular YouTube clip, she clearly articulates what the research had shown her: fitting in is assessing a group of people and changing who you are. And so fitting in is the opposite of belonging – true belonging never asks us to change who we are, it demands that we be who we are.[84]

This distinction is a fundamental one. And the importance of being yourself, and feeling like you can bring your whole self to the workplace, is backed up by the in-depth project that Google carried out back in 2012. Google had become focused on building the perfect team and in 2012, set up Project Aristotle to study the organization's hundreds of teams.[85] Researchers began by reviewing a half-century of academic studies looking at how teams worked. Were the best teams made up of people with similar interests or did it matter more whether everyone was motivated by the same kinds of rewards? Based on those studies, the researchers scrutinized the composition of groups inside Google. No matter how they arranged the data, it was impossible to find patterns.

As they struggled to figure out what made a team successful, the group kept coming across research by psychologists and sociologists that focused on what are known as 'group norms': the traditions, behavioural standards and unwritten rules that govern how we function when we gather. Project Aristotle's researchers began searching through the data they had collected, looking for norms. They then had to work out which were the norms that successful teams (which could look very different) shared. This built on research carried out in 2008 by psychologists from Carnegie Mellon, M.I.T. and Union College[86]. So, what did they discover? That the right 'norms' could raise a group's collective intelligence and that two

---

[84] https://www.youtube.com/watch?v=CgCRsfNNNyQ
[85] https://rework.withgoogle.com/print/guides/5721312655835136/
[86] http://www.cs.cmu.edu/~ab/Salon/research/Woolley_et_al_Science_2010-2.pdf

behaviours in particular were shared by the 'good' teams: equality of distribution in conversational turn taking and high 'average social sensitivity'.

The team felt that these findings aligned perfectly with a concept called 'psychological safety': a term coined by Harvard Business School professor Amy Edmondson, describing a group culture where there is a 'shared belief held by members of a team that the team is safe for interpersonal risk-taking'. A sense of confidence that the team will not embarrass, reject or punish someone for speaking up. A team climate characterized by interpersonal trust and mutual respect in which people are comfortable being themselves.

According to the powerful article on this in the *New York Times*, titled: 'What Google learned from its quest to build the perfect team'[87], what Project Aristotle taught people within Google is that no one wants to put on a 'work face' when they get to the office. No one wants to leave part of their personality and inner life at home.

Edmondson's work on psychological safety reinforces this fundamental distinction between fitting in and belonging. Fitting in will mean that you have left some of your personality at the door. It might get you so far. You might be able to perform for a period of time. But over the long term? Really performing to, and unleashing, your full potential? It's not going to happen. True belonging, however, will bring that feeling of safety, that ability to bring your whole self to the workplace. And as leader, why wouldn't you want that for your people?

[87] https://www.nytimes.com/2016/02/28/magazine/what-google-learned-from-its-quest-to-build-the-perfect-team.html

Fitting In versus Belonging

FITTING IN	BELONGING
• Aiming for acceptance;	• Feel accepted;
• Hiding true self;	• Able to be yourself;
• Feeling like an outsider;	• Feel like you belong;
• Not sustainable.	• Sustainable.

Lack of human connection

Back in 2015, some research was published that caught the attention of many people in sport. The paper was titled 'The Importance of Touch in Sport: Athletes' and Coaches' Reflections'. This study examined athletes' and coaches' experiences of positive touch within the coach-athlete relationship, including reasons for the use of touch and factors affecting athletes' acceptance of touch. All participants shared examples of positive touch in sport including hugs, high fives, physical manipulation of the body, pats on the back and hand shaking. Positive touch was reportedly used for affective, behavioural, safety and cultural reasons. Touch was viewed by these athletes and coaches as being important and even necessary in the sporting environment and within the coach-athlete relationship provided that it was individualized and contextualized.[88]

Despite what was a very small sample size, it was a significant study at the time because of the sensitivities around touch in child-centred domains. And it was tremendously important in reminding people of the positive aspects of touch in building human connection.

---

[88] https://www.researchgate.net/publication/279162697_The_Importance_of_Touch_in _Sport_Athletes'_and_Coaches'_Reflections

Human connection of course doesn't have to be through touch. It can be through verbal communication; through the time you give to someone, through the care you show. We will pick up on communication in more depth in the next chapter; at this stage it's worth sharing some insight from one of the most well-regarded coaches of modern times, Steve Kerr. Kerr is head coach of the Golden State Warriors in the NBA. After an incredibly successful playing career, taking in five NBA titles, he has continued this form as a coach, winning four titles to date with the Warriors. He has learned from the best (including Phil Jackson and Gregg Popovitch) and shared some of this wisdom in a clip posted on Twitter and shared among the coaching community. Kerr was asked about human connection and he said that both Phil and 'Pop' had taught him the need for the group to connect with one another and with the staff. He stated that the first order of business with any new player is to get to know them on a personal level and went on to assert that every person he had ever known responds to that human connection.[89]

Look back to the quote at the beginning of this chapter. This was shared with Cath Bishop, author of *The Long Win*[90]. In the book, Bishop examines our cultural obsession with winning and how it affects the way we approach work, sport, education and beyond. Great Britain international hockey player Alex Danson had won a Gold medal. At the Olympic Games. At her third time of asking. And yet what did she see as the most important thing? Human connection. And the COVID-19 pandemic has put even more of a spotlight on this need. In the McKinsey & Company article that we have already referenced (*see also* page 133), the authors go on to state that: 'If the past 18

---

[89] https://twitter.com/andrewbrownhil/status/1326484844654825474
[90] Cath Bishop, *The Long Win: The Search for a Better Way to Succeed*, Practical Inspiration Publishing, 2020.

months have taught us anything, it's that employees crave investment in the *human* aspects of work. They want a renewed and revised sense of purpose in their work. They want social and interpersonal connections with their colleagues and managers. They want to feel a sense of shared identity. Yes, they want pay, benefits, and perks, but more than that they want to feel valued by their organizations and managers. They want meaningful – though not necessarily in-person – *interactions*, not just transactions.'

And remember our initial story. When did Game Day end for London Pulse? Only *after* the post-match meal.

So how can we take all of this across into the workplace? How can you as leader drive this sense of belonging that will enable you to get the best out of your people on a sustained basis?

Getting the Best Out of Your People – On a Sustained Basis

Creating a clear sense of identity

Beyond a name, organizations are often timid when it comes to creating a clear sense of identity. Purpose is obviously fundamental here, as we have looked at already. And it is also where organizational values come into play. Organizations need to be bolder.

Netflix is an example of an organization that has been confident and clear about its DNA. In their publicly available culture statement, set out on their website, they are bold and unapologetic about what makes them different, what they stand for, what matters to them and how they operate. This isn't easy to do and requires a lot of discussion and reflection, however it is an incredibly powerful tool in fostering a strong feeling of belonging as it makes it very clear to everyone (internal and external) what it is they are belonging to. An example that is often shared from a slightly different time is that of Thomas Edison's 'muckers'. First coined as a term referring to the experiments carried out by Edison and his team around binding agents (or muck) for bricks, it came to also represent the element of trying and experimenting and getting stuck in (or mucking about) that the team wanted to encourage and preserve.

Take the time to consider what the identity of your organization is. Make sure you have clear organizational values. Reflect on what sort of attributes and behaviours are needed for your organization and don't be afraid to reinforce this on a consistent basis. Through your recruitment processes. Through your onboarding and induction processes. And through your reward and recognition framework.

One further point to note before we move on: we often read that companies should be like a family. That you should treat the people in your organization as if they were part of your family. I fundamentally disagree. Your organization is not like a family. With families, you don't get to choose who is in them – you do with your organization. Instead of a family, focus on creating a feeling of community, a clear sense of what that community stands for and what it does. Make sure it's open, warm and welcoming. Encouraging diversity and being as inclusive as possible. And if it's not right for someone, that's OK – people join and leave communities all the time.

Avoiding the 'fitting in' pitfall

To truly get the best out of your people over the long term, you have to let them be themselves. As we've just highlighted, not everyone is going to fit your organization. That's the way of the world. Once you are clear on what works for your organization, what your DNA is, try and make sure you have as diverse a set of people as possible for all the well-documented reasons. Be clear on what values and behaviours are important in your organization and then let them be. Let them feel included. Let them feel like they can be themselves. Let them feel like they belong. Do all you can to publicly celebrate the difference within your people, don't make them feel like they have to hide who they truly are in order to belong.

Driving human connection

Organizations have been facing the challenge of driving human connection with 'remote working' issues for a long time. It's nothing new. Think of all the global organizations out there who have hundreds of thousands of employees across continents. It's just that the COVID-19 pandemic has made this an issue for the vast majority of organizations, rather than a minority. So what kind of things should you be doing to drive human connection, particularly when not everyone is together all the time?

First, chunk things down. Do all you can to make sure that every person in your organization feels connected to someone else within the organization. And through that, to a team. And through that, perhaps to a unit. And through that, perhaps to a geographical location. And through that to the wider organization. Task the relevant managers with making this a priority within their areas of remit.

Second, at the senior level, with those with whom you will be working most closely, spend time getting to know them as a person: both at the recruitment stage and then as the relationship develops. A senior leader in a global law firm once shared with me the fact that before they recruit anyone at a senior level they have 14 different touch points – from initial interview to dinner out right through to a walk and talk. Lateral hires into law firms are notoriously difficult to get right, this gives them a much better chance of doing so.

Finally, with every conversation you have, make sure you put as much emphasis on connecting with that person as you do on the content of the conversation. It sounds so simple, but so often we focus on what we want to say and hear, not how we are interacting. One of the greatest gifts you can give to anyone is the gift of attention.

From the field of play to the corridors of leadership

Leila is the CEO of a large multinational charity. The charity has faced considerable challenge over the last two years, resulting in a reduced workforce. Leila has been concerned that her staff are losing faith in and commitment to the charity. She and her senior leadership team decide that one way to tackle this is to re-affirm a sense of belonging within the staff: a sense of faith in the organization, clarity on what it's all about, the vital role that everyone within it plays and the inter-connection and dependency between them all.

The purpose and vision of the organization are clear and compelling. Leila reminds herself that these need to be front and centre at all times. She is less sure of the continued relevance of the organization's values, so she instigates a process of sense-checking them. Through open invitations onto working groups at all levels and locations, a significant number of staff engage in the process. It becomes clear that the current articulations are no longer appropriate and over the next few months the working groups and project managers develop a new set of values. Once these have been signed off, Leila makes sure that these are embedded as well as possible and in particular that they are articulated, and repeated, at every available opportunity. All internal comms now have them on, as do much of their external comms. They have developed a page on their website where they clearly set out the DNA of the charity and use this in their recruitment process, onboarding and induction process, as well as reward and recognition processes.

Alongside this clarity on values, Leila and her senior leadership team focus on ensuring that throughout the organization her staff feel that they can bring their whole selves to the workplace and not feel like they have to work hard to fit in and be something that they are not. She consistently reinforces the message that while shared values are important in the organization, diversity of personality, perspective, experience and ways of thinking are crucial to driving the charity forwards. She has also worked hard with her director of HR to make sure there is a programme of events that ensure that every individual in the charity, no matter where they work from and how large or small their team, feels connected to each other and the wider organization.

In summary

- A sense of belonging is crucial to long-term, sustained performance.
- Creating a sense of identity for your organization is critical to facilitating a sense of belonging.
- Be bold and clear about the identity.
- Anchor this to your organization's purpose and values; people want to be part of something larger than themselves.
- Reinforce this externally and internally.
- Beware an environment of 'fitting in' rather than true belonging; you will get much more out of your people if they feel they can truly be themselves.
- Within the guardrails of your values, encourage and celebrate difference.
- Prioritize human connection; it's a powerful tool in fostering a sense of belonging.

CHAPTER TEN

How to Communicate with Positive Impact

'I'm a very strong believer in listening and learning from others.'

Ruth Bader Ginsburg, Former Associate Justice of the
Supreme Court of the United States

It's the evening of Friday, 19 August 2016. Rio de Janeiro is hosting the Olympic Games and tonight it's the turn of the women's hockey final. The final is being contested by reigning Olympic Champions the Netherlands and the Bronze medallists from London 2012, Great Britain. The Dutch are firm favourites on paper, although the GB squad have built up a fabulous momentum through the tournament.

Despite taking a shock early lead, the GB team soon finds itself 2–1 down. One of the players looks across at a teammate and sees that they are not in the right place mentally. The player knows she needs to help. But how can she communicate? They are in the middle of an Olympic final, focused on the play, pushing their bodies to the limit. The player probably has at most one or two seconds to get her message across – a message that needs to get that teammate back into the right place.

The player shouts one word. A well-chosen, well-practised word. Crisply. Clearly. And the impact is immediate. Her teammate lifts her head, re-focuses and is back in the game.

This process plays out over and over again throughout the final. Different players. Different words and phrases. All with the same impact. And against the odds, the GB team runs out eventual winners after a nail-biting penalty shoot-out finish.

This forensic ability to communicate the right words did not just happen. In the 2016 Olympic cycle, the squad had done a significant amount of work around self-awareness and knowledge of each other's strengths. They had also focused on learning the behaviours they exhibited when things were going well and those they exhibited when things were not going quite so well. And how specifically with what choice of words they could help each other move into a more positive state of mind. The precise and exhaustive work they did in this area paid off.

I wonder how often you have thought carefully about exactly what message you need to be communicating to those you lead? Whether you realize how powerful your communications are as a leader? What you say, and how you say it, has an increasingly significant impact the more senior you get. If you want to get the best out of those you lead, on a sustained basis, this is an area on which you really do need to spend some dedicated time.

How Do We Get This Wrong?

We've all seen this happen. You know when you yourself have got this wrong. Despite your best efforts, somehow you haven't seemed to get the right message across in the right way. Heads go down. Performance drops. And it's hard to bring it back up again. And this goes beyond the immediate moment. Our ability to communicate with positive impact, on a consistent basis, is central to our ability to engage and get the best out of those we lead over the long term. To drive performance in our people in a way that is sustainable.

What's behind this? What can we learn from the world of sport and take across into our leadership roles?

The big speech

If you have thought about the impact of your communications on those you lead, it's quite possible that much of your thinking has centred around the big speeches, the important moments. Where you feel it's important to deliver an inspiring and compelling message.

The story I'm about to share might have you thinking again.

Sam Walker is an editor for *The Wall Street Journal* with a passion for sport that borders on obsession. Several years ago, he set out to answer one of the most keenly debated questions in sport: what are the greatest teams of all time? Applying a detailed and complex formula, he identified the 16 most dominant teams across world sport. Having done this, he decided to try and answer the next most keenly debated question in sport – what is it about those teams that has made them so successful? What did they have in common which drove their sustained success? As Walker dug more deeply, a pattern emerged. One which surprised and even slightly annoyed him. Because what seemed to be the consistent factor was the captain in each of these teams. Somehow this seemed a bit too basic, a bit too easy.

The next surprise was in the characteristics of these captains. They differed in multiple ways from what our general perception is of a 'great' leader. One of these areas was how they communicated.

When we think of how to inspire performance in those we lead through our communication, the common image is that of a powerful speechmaker. Someone who can inspire and motivate through their compelling and influential words. This is not what Walker found though. As he says in his book, *The Captain Class*: 'It was here, in this regard, that the captains deviated the furthest from our image of what makes an eminent leader. These men and women were not silver-tongued orators or fiery motivators. They didn't like giving speeches. In fact, they made a point of avoiding them.'[91]

So, what is it that they did do? The answer was short-burst, high-energy communications. Not only this, they used much more than just words. They used tone. They used body language. And they made sure they were engaged, focused and energized.

Walker details some explosive insight from his ringside seat during a 2016 basketball game between the New Orleans Pelicans and the San Antonio Spurs (one of his top 16 teams). He had come to watch how captain Tim Duncan communicated with his players. Duncan was someone with a less-than-exciting public persona and certainly did not consider himself a vocal leader. Throughout the game, while on the surface the captain appeared contained and calm, what stood out for Walker was Duncan's eyes: he continually used them to communicate with his teammates and officials and convey powerful meaning. Whether that be shock (at a referee call), delivering a key message to a player or observing everything going on. Everything was calculated, all-powerful, he never broke eye contact and he listened as much as he talked.

When one player, Parker, was benched by the coach, Gregg Popovich, at the next break Duncan sprang into action. As Walker tells it, Duncan hurried off the court, walked straight over to Parker, put a hand on his head and lifted it up in order to lock eyes with him. Asking him 'You OK?' Once Parker had nodded, Duncan held the pose and gaze for about three seconds; only then did he take his seat.[92]

---

[91] Sam Walker, *The Captain Class: The Hidden Force Behind the World's Greatest Teams*, Ebury Press, 2017, p. 155.
[92] Sam Walker, *The Captain Class: The Hidden Force Behind the World's Greatest Teams*, Ebury Press, 2017, p. 167.

The different ways in which we communicate

Not only does the story above highlight the importance of consistent, regular, impactful communication, it also highlights the different ways in which we communicate. We communicate through three channels: verbals, non-verbals (body language) and tone. The impact of each of these is hotly contested (not least due to general misunderstanding of the initial research carried out in this area by Dr Albert Mehrabian, a pioneer researcher of body language in the 1950s); what is generally accepted is that all three channels have a powerful impact in terms of what messages people receive. And where these messages are conflicting, body language and tone can have a disproportionate effect. Imagine someone talking to you, delivering a gentle, kind message. If they are using an aggressive tone and aggressive body language alongside their words, it is likely that you will react more to the tone and body language than to the message.

The content

This brings us nicely onto the content of the message you are conveying. Imagine it's half-time in a high-pressure match. Your team is 1–0 down. It's a must-win game. The players are tired. You need to keep them in a challenge mindset, while delivering some key messages. There's two important points to bear in mind.

First, our brains can only take in and then execute on so much information. This is exacerbated when we are tired. The best coaches therefore tend to follow the 'rule of three' – making no more than three points during any crucial communication with their players.

Second, these points will need to be reinforced. *And* reinforced. *And* reinforced. To the extent that many coaches will talk about sounding like a broken record.

Keep it simple, keep it easy to understand and reinforce.

There is then a deeper level to this which finally made sense to me on reading a book by Bill McFarlan called *Drop the Pink Elephant*[93]. I once overheard a conversation between two cricket coaches. They were debating the best language to use to their batters as they went out to bat. One was in favour of what I would term negative language ('Don't lose your wicket early' or 'Don't be overly attacking') and the other was in favour of more positive language ('Concentrate throughout the innings', 'Stand tall' or 'Protect your wicket'). Instinctively, I felt that the latter would be more helpful and drive better performance from their players. This was reinforced in McFarlan's book and his brilliant articulation of what he called 'pink elephants' – the negatives which stay in our brains. If I say to a player, 'Don't lose your wicket early', what's going to stay in their brain? Losing their wicket early. The same goes for 'Don't be overly attacking'. I'm going to focus on the negative – not being overly attacking. What this tells us is that our choice of individual words is key, over the long term and in those high-pressure, in-the-moment conversations with our people.

Getting the Best Out of Your People – On a Sustained Basis

So, how can you make sure you get this right? And in a way that gets the best out of those you lead in a sustainable way?

Simple and tangible

It's easy to think, especially if you are a relatively inexperienced leader, that you need to sound like a leader. And for some this can mean an assumption that using over-sophisticated and complicated

---

[93] Bill McFarlan, *Drop the Pink Elephant: 15 Ways to Say What You Mean…and Mean What You Say,* Capstone Publishing Limited, 2004.

language is a must. The best leaders I know, however, speak clearly, simply and in a straightforward manner that people can understand. It's not about proving themselves, it's about helping their audience to take on the message. And they make sure that their message is tangible. Let's say my biggest challenge at the moment is to help my organization see how it fits into a larger ecosystem. I could try and explain this with lots of detail, big numbers and sophisticated language or I could work hard to distil my message down to something that is tangible. That way your people can properly understand what you are aiming for, giving them the clarity they need to engage productively and efficiently in working towards the right thing. Stories help, as do metaphors and visual images. Push yourself that bit harder to help your audience understand the message and take it on board.

Positive, not negative

For long-term performance from your people, you need your communications to have a positive effect. If you want to have a better chance of achieving this, use positive framing in your language. Remember that with every comment you are either adding to or taking away from, someone's performance. The words you use are going to be critical. 'Don't mess this up' will not be helpful, 'Focus on our strategic priorities' might be more so. The more consistently you are able to do this, the more consistent will be the performance from your people.

Body language and tone

It's important to be aware of what you are saying, when you are not actually saying it, so be careful. As leader, your communications carry disproportionate weight. Watch how you are delivering your message and what you are saying, not with your words, but with your tone and body language. You are much more likely to get sustained engagement and performance out of your people if your body language and tone align behind the positive intent of your words.

> 'I've learnt that people will forget what you said, people will forget what you did, but people will never forget how you made them feel.'

Maya Angelou, American poet and civil rights activist

Meet the recipients where they are at

Know your people. Know what works. Have you taken the time to understand the best way to deliver a message to the different individuals in your top team? Many top teams go through a behavioural assessment process (there are many available on the market) which can help them understand how best to communicate with each other and these can be used as a springboard for a more detailed conversation on what words and phrases work best with each individual. Who needs support? Who needs a bit more of a challenge? Just like the GB women's hockey squad.

More generally when communicating within the team, have you taken the time to consider when it's best to deliver an important message? At the beginning of the week or the end? In the middle of the day? At the start of a meeting or at the end? Take the time to think this through or even ask – it will help.

Consistency is king

We have all had that feeling when you've said something and 20 minutes later it seems like the person you were talking to never heard it. This is as relevant in your professional life as it is in your personal life.

Leaders need to sound like a broken record, i.e. repeating the same message. Each time you say it, you are increasing the chance of the message going in. And each time, you might be adding one more person to the list of those who have 'heard'. And that message has to be repeated in consistent terms, so that it's a consistent message.

I often use the following as a test when I go in and start working for organizations. If I stopped any employee in the lift, would they be able to articulate to me, accurately, the organization's vision? Its purpose? And can they tell me what the key strategic priorities are for this financial year? If they can't, it suggests to me that there has been a breakdown in communication, with most likely a significant lack of consistent repetition of a clear and unambiguous message.

Yes, messaging can be adapted and improved over time, but always work on the basis that you have to over-deliver your key messages rather than under-deliver on them to really make them stick. This is the way to ensure sustained performance over the long term.

Don't forget about listening

One of the insights that came out of Sam Walker's book, *The Captain Class* (see also page 148), was the importance of listening as well as speaking. Walker made the connection with some well-covered research conducted by Alex 'Sandy' Pentland and his team at the Human Dynamics Laboratory at the Massachusetts Institute of Technology (MIT). The team wanted to try and see if there was a science behind great teams. Spreading their research over 21 organizations across a range of sectors, they honed in on how they communicated and how those communication patterns influenced their performance. Each team member was given a 'badge' – a wireless multimedia recorder worn like a name tag that took digital images and recorded audio. These could pick up tone of voice, body language, who they talked to and so on.

Researchers isolated the data signatures of what Pentland referred to as the 'natural leaders', whom the scientists called charismatic connectors. Pentland wrote that the data showed that these people circulate actively, engaging others in short, high-energy conversations. He highlighted that they were not necessarily extroverts, listened as much or more than they talk and were usually very engaged with whomever they were listening to.[94]

And in uncertain times ...

Many leaders fast-tracked their skillset around communication during the COVID-19 pandemic. One of the key questions to consider was what, and how much, to communicate. And the tendency for many, at least in the early stages, was to under-communicate due to lack of concrete information and answers. However, this is dangerous. Where there is a vacuum, it tends to get filled. With assumptions. With incorrect information. And with ever-increasing panic. And this is not conducive to sustained and effective performance.

What leaders soon realized was that a steady stream of communication, even if they didn't have all the answers, helped. It helped to keep people calm. It bred confidence. It made them feel like they were all in it together. It also steadied the ship, at least giving a semblance of calm. And in uncertain times, perception is key.

The learning to take forward is not to hide, not to retreat, not to safely stay quiet when things are uncertain. So, step up, provide whatever certainty you can and make sure that everyone knows you are all in it together.

---

[94] Sam Walker, *The Captain Class: The Hidden Force Behind the World's Greatest Teams*, Ebury Press, 2017, p. 161 and https://hbr.org/2012/04/the-new-science-of-building-great-teams

From the field of play to the corridors of leadership

Sue is a first-time CEO. Keen to set herself good habits from the start, she knows her people are her most important asset and is really focused on getting sustainable performance from those she is leading. Before she began the role, she approached her mentor (Chris) and asked him for three key bits of advice. Along with suggestions on the importance of prioritization and embedding a growth mindset, he highlighted the importance of communication. Chris stressed that now Sue was CEO, her communications would carry even greater weight. She should think carefully about everything she said and communicated, from big presentations right through to her comments to someone while passing them in the corridor.

Sue had never really thought too carefully about the language she used. At her previous organization she was aware of having felt the need to live up to the CEO, who was brilliant at delivering inspirational speeches. She hadn't really thought before about the day-to-day. A month later, Sue had an experience that really highlighted this for her. One of her leadership team had an important meeting coming up. This person came to see Sue, to ask for her advice and guidance. She was particularly busy at that moment and didn't think carefully enough about what she said so she reeled off what she hoped would be valuable insight for her colleague. On reflection she realized it had been woolly advice, not simple and concrete enough, probably confusing, and that she certainly had not given this colleague her full time and attention. And her body language would have made this very clear.

Unfortunately, the meeting did not go well and this had a significant impact on the fortunes of the business over the next three months. Sue told herself after that incident that she needed to think much more carefully about how and what she communicated, and in particular the need to be clear, to give her full attention to a conversation, listen properly and to set out and reinforce simple, consistent messages. If she had done this, she would have helped her colleague in a much better way, leading to a much better result.

She decided to focus on developing her ability in this area, particularly with her leadership team, with whom she has now gone through a behavioural profiling process with an external consultant. This process has helped them all understand how best to communicate with each other. Off the back of this Sue learnt that her finance director prefers detailed, well-structured information and instructions, while her chief operating officer prefers concise, to-the-point communications. Her marketing director prefers support words and her sales director prefers challenge words. Sue and the team have found this invaluable in getting the best out of each other on a consistent basis.

In summary

- How and what you communicate as a leader has a significant and disproportionate impact on performance.
- Inspirational and powerfully constructed speeches have their place and some leaders have this as a super-strength, but they are not the be-all and end-all.

- To drive long-term, sustained performance, it's more about consistent, regular, energetic, positive, simple and impactful interactions.
- In every situation think carefully about your choice of words and body language and tone.
- Listening is an important, and powerful, form of communication.
- Remember your growth mindset from Chapter 1 (*see also* pages 20–30) – this underpins your ability to improve in every area.
- Be consistent in, and consistently reinforce, your message.
- Keep it simple, tangible and clear.
- Know your people – know what works for them.
- Beware under-communicating in situations of uncertainty and pressure.

CHAPTER ELEVEN

How to Develop Your People in a Long-Term Way

'A good coach can change a game. A great coach can change a life.'

John Wooden, American basketball coach

In Sweden's far north, a group of people are waiting to go out on stage and perform. Part of their performance involves a rendition of *Swan Lake*, the ballet. The troupe is half-excited, half-nervous. This would be normal were they seasoned performers. The fact that they are professional footballers makes this somewhat extraordinary.

The troupe are members of Östersund FK's football squad, led by English coach Graham Potter. And this performance is, almost unbelievably, not out of character. For the squad had already grown used to performing significantly outside of their comfort zone, taking in plays, ballets, rap performances and even writing books. So how does a bunch of (male) football players find themselves performing *Swan Lake* on stage to the local population of their small town in Sweden?

The year 2010 was a defining one for Östersund FK. For the first time ever, they were relegated to the fourth tier of Swedish football. The club was shaken; most of the Board resigned and many of the players left too. It was time for drastic change. With little money, and a challenging location (a seven-hour drive from Stockholm and further still from Gothenburg), they had to find a different way to engineer a turnaround. The Board sat down and planned out an ambitious strategy to get the team to the Allsvenskan (the top tier of Swedish football) and eventually qualify for Europe. Part of this strategy was a bold and unorthodox plan to establish a Culture Academy at the club. The Academy would work with players and staff in areas outside their comfort zones (music, theatre, ballet), help them develop as human beings and, ultimately, they believed, improve the team's chances of victory on the pitch. They presented their vision to the club's then-chairman Daniel Kindberg who, along with head coach Graham Potter, embraced the idea enthusiastically. And so the Culture Academy was born.

The fact that the club was operating to a large extent below the radar definitely helped in being able to get this off the ground. The impact in terms of results though was what propelled its continuation and subsequent development; the turnaround in performance of the team was remarkable. By 2015, the club had been promoted to the Allsvenskan, then in 2017, they managed to win their first major trophy, the Svenska Cupen, also qualifying for the 2017/18 UEFA Europa League, marking their first appearance in a European competition tournament. They qualified for the Group Stage at the first time of asking, at the same time making them the only Swedish representative in the season's UEFA competition and Graham Potter the only British manager in the Europa League Group Stage.

Amazing success for a small, remote club in Sweden, competing with the long-established, much wealthier, big clubs of Europe, but it hasn't all been plain sailing for Östersund, with Potter having moved on and Chairman Daniel Kindberg having been convicted (though later acquitted) of financial impropriety. And their turnaround has not been exclusively down to the Culture Academy. Their journey does though reflect a decision to do things differently, with a strong focus on really valuing and investing in their people, and developing them in a broader and more long-term way. As Club Secretary Lasse Landin shared in 2019, talking about putting the players in positions that were entirely new (and uncomfortable) for them: 'At first, all new players and staff are apprehensive of what we do because it's a new experience for them. It's about doing things you're not used to doing. No other club has done this type of thing before, so everyone starts off like a little child – they have to learn to crawl first, then walk and finally perform.'[95]

This focus on valuing their players as people and looking to develop them accordingly is particularly relevant at the moment. In Chapter 9, I referenced a McKinsey & Company article that examined what towards the end of 2021 was being termed the Great Resignation (*see also* page 133). The article starts with a significant statement: more than 19 million US workers had quit their jobs since April 2021. The authors go on to explore the reasons why, with their research showing that not feeling valued by their organizations came out top, at 54 per cent.[96]

I have been linking this in my own mind with the message that several senior leaders have been sharing with me over the last couple of years: employees are making it clear that they want to be valued and developed in a more rounded way. And I have seen this first-hand through a groundbreaking movement in the legal sector. The O Shaped Lawyer was set up in 2019 by a group of General Counsel (GCs) who felt strongly that the lawyers they were instructing were not fit for purpose. While strong technical lawyers, they did not have the more rounded skills that were now required by their clients: attributes like courage, empathy and resilience. The movement has swiftly gained traction throughout the legal sector in the UK (and beyond) with O Shaped now working with law schools right through to global law firms to help embed more rounded skillsets within legal professionals.[97]

[95] https://sustainabilityreport.com/2019/08/12 /how-ostersunds-fks-culture-academy-blazed-a-trail-for-sporting-success/
[96] https://www.mckinsey.com/business-functions/people-and-organizational-performance/our-insights/great-attrition-or -great-attraction-the-choice-is-yours
[97] https://www.oshaped.com/

So, what are the lessons we can take from sport and how can you deploy them into your leadership? What is it about the approach that the best clubs and coaches, those that develop their players for the long term, take? And how is it that we so often get this wrong?

How Do We Get This Wrong?

Not developing the person as well as the player

The story above sheds light on an issue that many organizations miss: the importance of developing their people in ways that go over and above their job description. In order both to broaden their perspective and expertise and to keep them challenged and engaged.

We have explored already in this book the careers of Venus and Serena Williams (*see also* page 57). They were coached by their father, Richard Williams. Williams senior took a rather unusual approach to their development in a variety of different ways. One of the areas in which he deviated from the norm was in how he encouraged the development of a broader range of interests in his girls, alongside their tennis. This is something that the author David Epstein has written about extensively. Epstein argues in his book *Range: How Generalists Triumph in a Specialized World*[98] that modern life requires range. The ability to make connections across domains and ideas. That bringing experience and perspective from other areas can enhance your performance over the long term. Just as playing a variety of different sports can actually enhance your ability in your main one over the long term. And he reinforces this point in a recent piece on Serena Williams, sharing the story of the day he came face to face with her as an audience member in one of his talks. Finishing his speech, Williams was the first to put her hand up to ask a question. To Epstein's immense relief and delight, she further

---

[98] David Epstein, *Range: How Generalists Triumph in a Specialized World*, Macmillan, 2019.

reinforced the point he had been making on the benefits of variety. She gave the audience a first-hand account of the variety of activities she had participated in as a child: ballet, gymnastics, taekwondo and track and field. And she made this very powerful point: 'I think my father was ahead of his time.'[99]

Range. Giving Serena and Venus a better chance of performing well over the long term. Remaining more interested by, and engaged with, their tennis. Because it wasn't the only thing they were doing. And also driving their performance on the tennis court due to the positive impact the other activities had on their core sport.

And for athletes who have played a variety of sports while their progress might be slower, they can potentially bring more to the table over the longer term; seeing patterns, benefiting from the different skillsets. Earlier in the chapter we came across Lasse Landin, Secretary of Östersund FK (*see also* page 160). In terms of the Cultural Academy's impact on improved performance over time, he said this: 'In football, you have to be brave and know how to think and how others are thinking, including both your own teammates and the opposition. The Academy is one way of making the players and staff braver and more creative, which in turn will make them better at decision-making.'[100]

And to reinforce the point, there are two aspects to the impact this has on long-term performance. Not just improved ability, but also better and more sustained motivation. Think back to Chapter 4, where we looked at what drives motivation over the long term (*see also* pages 57–71) We explored the issue of elite athletes performing better when they had something other to concentrate on than just their sport. Remember Claire Taylor, the cricketer, whose pursuit of interests (and indeed a whole other job) outside her sport propelled

[99] https://davidepstein.bulletin.com/that-time-serena-williams-made-my-day/
[100] https://sustainabilityreport.com/2019/08/12/how-ostersunds-fks-culture-academy-blazed-a-trail-for-sporting-success/

her cricket career forwards? Remember Professor Lavallee suggesting that this issue of greater breadth is where the performance gains will be seen in elite sport over the next 20 years. Outside of tennis, Serena Williams has not only spent time building and developing her fashion knowledge, including launching her own fashion line in 2018, she has also set up her own venture capital firm, Serena Ventures. Venus Williams has also pursued an interest in fashion, gaining an Associate Degree in Fashion Design from the Art Institute of Fort Lauderdale in 2007, adding to this with a Bachelor of Science degree in Business Administration from Indiana University East in 2015. Developing the person as well as the player equals better long-term performance and we need to do more of this in today's world.

Where else do we go wrong in how we develop our people?

Not getting coaching right

In 2019 Herminia Ibarra and Anne Scoular published an article in *Harvard Business Review* titled 'The Leader as Coach'. The premise was that in today's uncertain and rapidly changing world, managers don't (and can't) have all the right answers. To cope with this new reality, companies are moving away from traditional command-and-control practices and towards something very different: a model in which managers give support and guidance rather than instructions and employees learn how to adapt to constantly changing environments in ways that unleash fresh energy, innovation and commitment – in short, where they are acting as a coach.

The authors go on to make one very powerful point: **you are not as good as you think**. They quote one study where 3,761 executives assessed their own coaching skills and then their assessments were compared with those of people who worked with them. The results didn't align well: 24 per cent of the executives significantly overestimated their abilities, rating themselves as above average, while their colleagues ranked them in the bottom third of the group. That's a telling mismatch. 'If you think you're a good coach but you actually aren't,' the authors of the study wrote, 'this data suggests you may be a good deal worse than you imagined.'[101]

In sport, there is a vast variety of coaching ability on offer. It is a skill that needs to be learnt, developed and built. And this is in a domain where coaching ability is the main requirement for the job! It stands to reason, then, that to develop this skillset in a management/ leadership role, this needs to be focused on, rather than just being a by-product of the wider role.

Only half the story

One key way in which many leaders fall down is in not structuring their coaching conversations in the right way. We examined in Chapter 8 the formula of High Standards plus Assurance (*see also* page 128). The message to people that you have high standards and expectations and that you are confident that they will achieve them. Imagine I'm the coach of an Olympic team and I use this formula when speaking to an athlete. I tell them that we have very high standards within our set-up, that we have high expectations of them as an individual athlete and that we are confident that they will achieve them. And I leave it at that. What does that athlete go away with? Perhaps they feel more confident. Perhaps they feel that I believe in them. Perhaps they feel happy. There is, however, another possibility: that I have left them feeling incredibly frustrated. This athlete wants to make the Olympic team. There are more athletes vying for the team than there are places. The athlete is worried about their ability to secure their spot on the team. So, while my intention as the coach might have been to lift them up, I have perhaps inadvertently done

---

[101] https://hbr.org/2019/11/the-leader-as-coach

the opposite of helping them. Why? Because I have given them the dream, without giving them the tools and information they need to reach it. I have not given them direction and I have not shown them where they need to, and can, obtain support.

If only, after my assertion of their ability, I had continued the conversation. If only I had perhaps said, 'At the moment you are a strong prospect for the team. There are some particular aspects however that you need to continue to work on and develop. In the next month you need to focus on "x". And in order to help you develop your capabilities in this area, I'm going to set up a meeting for you with "y", who can set the right plan for you,' then I'd most probably have a happier athlete. I'd certainly have an athlete who has much better clarity on what needs improving and how to go about it. And I would definitely be demonstrating an enhanced ability to develop them in a long-term way.

Let's now look at one other way in which leaders really get it wrong when it comes to coaching.

Irregular and guarded feedback

Too many organizations still rely on infrequent and irregular feedback. Annual performance reviews, with perhaps a half-year check-in at best. If I'm that athlete wanting to get into the Olympic team, that's not going to cut it for me. I want regular, consistent feedback to help me plot my progress, to understand where I still need to be improving. And I need it to be honest and clear. Too often we hold off giving feedback because we worry that we might upset the other person; in fact, we are doing them a disservice. If you want your people to improve and develop, and so remain engaged, motivated and productive over the long term, regular and consistent feedback is key. The mindset shift is at the crux of this: ensuring your people understand that feedback they receive is given for their benefit and that those giving feedback are helping and supporting the recipient to continually develop and improve.

Sport is a brilliant vehicle to demonstrate the importance of this mindset and the benefits of regular, consistent, clear and candid feedback. And this is an area where I see one of the biggest gaps between organizations' beliefs about their performance and the reality. When working with organizations, I sometimes bring in elite athletes as guest presenters, knowing that they can get certain messages across in a powerful way. The area where I do this most consistently is when talking about feedback. I have watched many times the faces of an audience while listening to Crista Cullen, member of the winning GB hockey squad (and veteran of four Olympic campaigns) explain the approach they took to feedback in the Rio Olympic cycle. The squad had a traffic light system, where the players would be faced with a traffic light as they entered the room for their regular feedback sessions; the light would indicate how likely it was, at that moment in time, that they would be on the plane to Rio. This was critical, as from a training squad of 31 players, only 19 players would be getting on the plane. A green would indicate 'You're on the plane', an orange 'You are in contention' and a red 'At the moment it is not likely that you are doing enough to get you on that plane' – with of course appropriate support and direction given accordingly. The story always hits home. It helps the audience understand who feedback is for (the recipient), why it's vital to ensure that it's delivered in a regular and clear fashion and how it can benefit the recipient to achieve their goals.

Not embedding a true learning culture

All of this is predicated on an understanding of the value of a true learning culture and an understanding of how to properly embed this. The best sports clubs and coaches have a focus on continuous learning, continuous development, knowing this is what will drive their sustained success.

And in business? Satya Nadella became only the third-ever CEO in Microsoft's history when he took over from Steve Ballmer in 2014. The company was struggling. From the dizzy heights of Bill Gates' tenure, they were now at risk of not just lagging behind, but becoming irrelevant. Nadella knew he had to change things: fast and dramatically. After his own period of listening and learning, he started to lay out his plans for change. The company itself had stopped listening. The company had stopped learning. The company had stopped being open to improvement. At the annual global sales conference, in front of 15,000 people, Nadella closed out his speech by talking about culture. Because, as he said to the audience: 'To me it is everything.'

And he continued with the following: 'We can have all the bold ambitions. We can have all the bold goals. We can aspire to our new mission. But it's only going to happen if we live our culture, if we teach our culture. And to me that model of culture is not a static thing. It is about a dynamic learning culture. In fact, the phrase we use to describe our emerging culture is "growth mindset", because it's about every individual, every one of us, having that attitude – that mindset – of being able to overcome any constraint, making it possible for us to grow, and, thereby, for the company to grow.'[102]

Inspirational words. Did they have an impact? Did they drive change on the ground? As Nadella went on to say in his book, 'After three years of intensive focus on culture-building we began to see some encouraging results.' Three years. Involving detailed and organization-wide training and coaching, alongside system and process change. With a constant reiteration and demonstration of the message from the top.

---

[102] Satya Nadella, *Hit Refresh, The Quest to Rediscover Microsoft's Soul and Imagine a Better Future for Everyone*, William Collins, 2018, pp. 93–4.

So what can you, as a leader, take from this insight? What practical steps should you be taking?

Getting the Best Out of Your People – On a Sustained Basis

Develop your people in a broader way

Organizations need people to be skilled at their jobs. To have the right capabilities, skillsets and attributes. And for the individual, sufficient focus and dedication enables them to build and develop towards mastery of their role. This doesn't mean however that they can't also develop in other areas; develop other, related skillsets; broaden out their spheres of understanding. And in fact, this can enhance their performance, and mastery, over the long term. One of the best examples of this that I have come across is the legal team of a large financial institution. At the beginning of each week, a member of the team brings some insight and knowhow to the team meeting. While it can be linked to the law, they are encouraged to focus on topics and areas that are tangential, relevant, useful, but not directly about the law. After the knowledge share, each team member goes away and finds five follow-up pieces of insight on the topic and each of them shares this at the team meeting at the end of the week. It's a brilliant way to engage, motivate and develop your people in a way that goes beyond the short term. And in a way that ensures that they each bring a richer and deeper set of skills, attributes and knowledge to their roles.

Other organizations support their people in learning and development that very much sits outside of their day jobs. Actively encouraging their staff to apply for funding in areas that develop them as a person, rather than just as someone who fills a particular role. Team away days where the activities take people out of their comfort zones, where they learn new things about themselves and their teammates, again can be a good tool to use in this area. Just think back to the players in Östersund

FK's squad. Think how much they learn about themselves and their teammates when they are so far out of their comfort zones in their Culture Academy activities. And how clear they are about the positive impact this has on their performance on the pitch.

Getting coaching right

Use of the HEADS framework

There are some tools which consistently get the thumbs up, no matter with whom I am sharing them. The HEADS framework is one of these:

I use this as it's easier to remember and it's derived from the formula shared by Dan and Chip Heath in their book, *The Power of Moments*[103]. In any coaching moment, keeping this framework in mind ensures that you set the scene in the right way, give yourself the best chance of them listening and then give them the concrete help and guidance that they can benefit from. Practise this until it becomes second nature.

The right messages at the right times

Giving feedback, sharing insight, reviewing performance ... these aren't things that should be happening only on a formal and spaced out timetable. If you want to truly get the best out of your people and drive long-term, sustained improvement and performance, you should be looking for coaching moments every single day. Ensuring that these are regular, consistent and honest. Watch a sports coach in action with their player or team and they find these coaching moments all the time,

---

[103] Chip and Dan Heath, *The Power of Moments,* Bantam Press, 2017.

making sure they don't lose the golden opportunity to deliver a message or trigger some insight at the time when it's most likely to land. Leaders should be doing the same: don't lose the power of the moment.

It's also important to recognize and understand what that particular person needs at that time. We have come across Mel Marshall already (*see also* page 27). She is the coach of the fastest breaststroke swimmer in the world, Adam Peaty, and has coached him since he was 14. Marshall once described her ability to adapt her coaching to the needs of the person in front of her in a way which has always stayed with me: front, side and back coaching. When Peaty was young, Marshall needed to coach him from the front. He needed to be led and guided in quite a directive way. As he matured and developed, she could start to coach alongside him. Now that Peaty is an experienced and very mature swimmer, Marshall coaches from the back, supporting, facilitating, encouraging and stepping in as needed. The model aligns well with the model which Ibarra and Scoular use in their article (*see also* page 164), where they make the distinction between directive, non-directive and situational coaching.

Ensuring the culture, systems and processes support this

As Ibarra and Scoular highlight, to transform your culture into a genuine learning culture, you need to make coaching an organizational capacity that fits integrally within your company culture.

First, just as at Microsoft, you need to emphasize the 'Why'. In sport, it's a straightforward and clear link: I am coaching you so that you can improve as an athlete and achieve your dreams. Outside of sport, the link can be slightly less obvious so it's vital to connect this to the organization's priorities. The senior partner of one law firm understood this and came up with a brilliant pitch for the 'Why'. As Scoular and Ibarra note, when David Morley, then senior partner of global law firm Allen & Overy, decided to make coaching a key part of the firm's leadership culture, he used the following pitch: 'As a senior leader, you have roughly 100 conversations a year that are of particularly high value – in the sense that they will change your life or the life of the person you're talking to. We want to help you acquire the skills to maximize value in those 100 conversations, to unlock previously hidden issues, to uncover new options and to reveal fresh insights.' That resonated. Almost everybody in a key leadership position at the firm recognized that they struggled with how to make the most of those conversations and they could readily see that they lacked skills.

Second, you need to lead from the top in role modelling a growth mindset. In *Think Again*, Adam Grant shares a story which highlights the power of this. Working with the Gates Foundation, helping them drive a learning environment and psychological safety, he encouraged Melinda Gates to share a video where she sat in a hot seat, read out note cards on which her team had compiled criticism of her from staff surveys and reacted. Gates demonstrated confident humility. She explained how she was trying to work on some of her imperfections and laughed out loud at some of the things written down. She engaged with the tough comments. And the impact? The listeners came away with a stronger learning orientation. It also led to some of the power distance evaporating, something which is critical to making sure honest and constructive feedback travels upwards as well as downwards.[104]

Third, you need to upskill all your managers and leaders in how to have coaching conversations. Make this a priority. Take this seriously.

Fourth, ensure your organization's values are carefully-chosen and articulated – they should drive everything that happens in the organization. More on this in the next chapter.

Finally, make sure your systems and processes support and drive growth mindsets and a learning culture. Set up learning forums. Be

---

[104] Adam Grant, *Think Again: The Power of Knowing What You Don't Know*, WH Allen, 2021, pp. 214–15.

disciplined on your review process after each and every project. Build learning goals into your reward and recognition schemes. Emphasize it in induction, emphasize it in recruitment. In short, make sure it's a thread that goes throughout everything that happens in your organization.

From the field of play to the corridors of leadership

Paula was director of people at a medium-sized financial organization. The business was doing well, however there were a number of disruptors to their business model on the horizon and she realized that they would only be able to navigate them if the business developed much more of a coaching and learning culture.

Paula's first priority was to get the CEO on board. She knew that without her close support and sponsorship, this would not be a success. Paula and her CEO spent some time discussing the Microsoft Model Coach Care framework that she had recently read about: the framework that Microsoft asks all of its leaders to follow in order to embed a growth mindset at the organizational level. Paula then developed a two-year plan which included a focus on the following:

- training for the senior leadership team on growth mindset;
- agreement and adoption of a framework that worked for them, using the Microsoft one as a guide;
- a revisit of the organization's values to check and challenge if they were the right ones;
- clear messaging from the top on the importance of a continuous focus on learning in working towards the organization's vision and goals;

- training for all managers to upskill them with the appropriate coaching skillset;
- processes and systems in place to ensure all teams run learning forums, with a focus on cross-fertilization of these across the organization; and
- changes to the recruitment, induction and onboarding, and reward and recognition schemes to ensure and reflect the emphasis on learning, including the institution of learning goals alongside outcome goals.

In summary

- Prioritize the development of your people – it benefits them, it benefits the organization.
- Sport knows that if you develop the person, as well as the player, you get more sustained performance over the long term. Leaders should be doing the same.
- A coaching approach is central to developing your people in a long-term way; it doesn't just happen however, it takes time and attention.
- Be clear on the 'Why' and link it to the organizational goals.
- Get support and sponsorship from the top.
- Build a coaching skillset at all the right levels.
- Look for coaching moments each and every day.
- Remember the purpose of feedback: helping and supporting the recipient to continually develop and improve.
- Ensure your culture, systems and processes support this focus on coaching, learning and improving.

CHAPTER TWELVE

How to Make Your Values Count

'The standard you walk past is the standard you become.'

Ben Ryan, coach and elite performance specialist

Don't leave your water bottle on the pitch. This was a lesson learnt the hard way by members of the England Women's football team in 2018.

The beginning of that year had marked a significant change for the team, known as the Lionesses. Phil Neville was appointed manager and brought with him a distinct shift in style. Neville had played with huge success under the legendary Sir Alex Ferguson at Manchester United, before spending eight years at Everton. He then moved on to a coaching career, which began with the England Under-21 team and then took in a couple of club roles before being appointed to lead the Lionesses.

Neville was chosen in part because of the mix of discipline and empathy that he could bring to the squad. After all, he had learnt from the best: Alex Ferguson was renowned for getting the most out of his players through a culture of discipline balanced with a genuine care for them (much as he usually hid this well with his fairly gruff manner). Family life had also instilled in Neville an appreciation for the importance of standards, something that has stood all three siblings in good stead through their careers: brother Gary, fellow Manchester United and England footballer, now a renowned and well-respected pundit and twin sister Tracey, former England netball international, former England head coach and just recently appointed second assistant at Adelaide Thunderbirds. In fact, twins Phil and Tracey hold a pretty unique record, both coaching their respective England sides to World Cup semi-finals in the same year (2019).

One of the early stories that came out of the England camp, reflecting the change in style and approach under Neville, was the water bottle saga. While overseas, the squad had taken part in a training session. The session finished, the players and support staff boarded the bus and the bus pulled away. It was at this point that Neville noticed something that caused him to stop the bus: someone had left a water bottle on the pitch. The culprit was identified, they exited the bus, picked up the bottle, re-joined the bus and off they all went. Why this fuss over one small water bottle? Because it represented something bigger for Neville: it was about upholding the standards and behaviour that he wanted to see at every moment. Why should the water bottle be left for the kit man to pick up?

In the previous chapter we looked at some of the words that Microsoft's Satya Nadella shared with his sales force as he was re-booting the organization (*see also* page 168). He made some bold statements externally as well. In 2015, he stated at the AGM that: 'our ability to change our culture is the leading indicator of our future success.'[105] He knew that changing culture wasn't just about words. It wasn't just about carefully crafted value statements. It was about the reality on the ground. The consistent, day in, day out behaviours that were displayed. And it was this that would determine the success or otherwise of the company.

Values take you so far, but it's only the start.

---

[105] https://www.ft.com/content/39db7e82-3947-11ea-ac3c-f68c10993b04

Sport has long understood that behind a carefully worded set of values must sit an equally carefully agreed set of behaviours that help people to understand what the values actually mean. How they should be behaving. What they should be prioritizing. What's acceptable and what isn't. Without this, values are just a well-intended set of words that sit on walls, screensavers and websites, not having any impact at all. With this, you significantly enhance your chances of ensuring sustained, consistent performance from your people.

This is why, despite the continued discussion and debate about how we truly define organizational culture, my favourite articulation remains the following: 'An organization's culture is the combined result of the values, attitudes and behaviours exhibited in its engagement with stakeholders both internal and external'.[106]

So, what can we learn from sport? What should we be avoiding and how can we make our values count and thereby ensure consistent, sustained performance from our people?

How Do We Get This Wrong?

The two leadership pitfalls on culture

From all I have read and seen, I believe that there are two pitfalls on culture that leaders must avoid: under-playing their hand and over-playing their hand.

Underplaying your hand

For many leaders, strategy is a comfort zone. It's tangible. It can be clearly written down and communicated. It provides a plan, which can then be executed on. The fundamentals of strategy are relatively

---

[106] Birkbeck University of London, Moore Stephens, 'The State of Sports Governance: Are you leading or lagging?'

easy to understand. The people element of an organization can often be more challenging; again though there is something reassuringly tangible about it. Making sure you have the right people in the right roles. With the right skillsets. Within a structure that aligns to the strategy of the organization. Human nature might throw up issues and challenges, they are though in general visible, palpable and describable.

Culture tends to be a different beast. Leaders are often confounded by culture. It is much more likely to push them out of their comfort zone made up as it is of the less tangible, the harder to pin down and describe, the more nebulous. The danger with this is that leaders too often underplay their hand in this area. They lack confidence, lack knowledge, lack understanding and so let it go unmanaged or relegate it to the HR function, often through this immediately signifying a lack of importance. And yet unless your culture is aligned with your strategy, you are not going to be able to achieve your goals. Your culture matters. Not just to current performance, but to sustained performance as well. And what too many leaders fail to appreciate is the significance of their role in this. The title of psychologist, author and former professional basketball player John Amaechi's book on leadership sums up the point brilliantly: *The Promises of Giants*[107]. As leader, everything you do has disproportionate impact. No matter how large the organization, the leaders set the tone: what you do matters more than others.

As leaders, you should play the hand you have. Understand that people will look to you for what's acceptable and what isn't. For how they should behave. For what the organizational values really mean in practice. And don't just pass the ball to others in the organization.

---

[107] John Amaechi OBE, *The Promises of Giants: How YOU Can Fill the Leadership Void*, Nicholas Brealey Publishing, 2021.

In *Hit Refresh*, Satya Nadella makes the bold statement that he thinks the 'C' in CEO stands for culture. Because he believes the CEO is the curator of an organization's culture and that creating the right kind of culture was and is his chief job as CEO.[108]

And it's not just about *your* behaviour, it's also about the behaviour that you walk past. As that wonderful saying goes: the standard you walk past is the standard you accept. 'Culture' will happen whether you like it or not. If you stand back and disengage, you leave it to chance and so run the risk of a culture developing that is contrary to what the business needs, that is not aligned with strategy: you need to play your hand.

Over-playing your hand

The other pitfall for leaders in this area is over-playing your hand. Yes, you have a significant role to play. Yes, you need to be constantly aware both of what you are doing and what you are saying. But to ensure a culture that is truly established and embedded, that has a life beyond the short term, it needs to be continually shaped and enforced by your people. It needs to be self-policing. Talk to any coach, from the U-9s local soccer team to elite national coaches, and they will all reinforce the same thing: you only know that the culture is truly established when the players call each other out, when they are the ones who notice a behaviour that doesn't fit the team values and deal with it.

And it's not just in this area where you need to be aware of over-playing your hand. Where leaders are involved in a culture change process and with this the setting of new values, beware the pitfall of having made up your mind before you start. Of having answered the

---

[108] Satya Nadella, *Hit Refresh: The Quest to Rediscover Microsoft's Soul and Imagine a Better Future for Everyone*, William Collins, 2018 p. 100.

question before it's even been set. That U-9 soccer team? The right coach will know that involving them in the process of agreeing the team's values and behaviours for the season will make it much more likely that the values will actually count. That their behaviour on the ground will reflect them. And that their values and behaviours are aligned with what it is they are trying to achieve that season, giving them a much better chance of success, whatever they want that to look like.

A leader can be clear on the culture they want to see and also clear on the role that they play in this but too often I see leaders over-playing their hand. Taking over. Taking control. Deciding on what it should look like without involving others. Building a sustainable culture takes much more than just the leader setting it and enforcing it.

UK Coaching (https://www.ukcoaching.org/) is there to support the 3 million coaches in the UK (voluntary and paid). One of the significant assets of the organization is the knowhow they share through their online Connected Coaches community. In the many threads on setting values and behaviours, one theme is consistent throughout: the importance of involving the players in the process.

If 9-year-old children are trusted to do this, surely you can trust your own people? Especially when you know that in doing so you are much more likely to make your values count.

Values, not driving action

Not being clear or actionable

What's the purpose of your organizational values? See if you can answer that question in one or two sentences.

Done it? Hopefully your answer includes something around guiding everything that happens within your organization. Your values are (or should be) the principles that govern every decision, every behaviour, every process, every recruitment, every promotion. In order for this to happen, values need to be clear and actionable. 'Inclusion' is not a value. 'Prioritizing inclusion in all we do' is. 'Resilience' is not a value. 'Being Resilient' is. As Simon Sinek wrote in *Start With Why: How Great Leaders Inspire Everyone to Take Action*, 'for values or guiding principles to be truly effective they have to be verbs. It's not "integrity," it's "always do the right thing." It's not "innovation," it's "look at the problem from a different angle." Articulating our values as verbs gives us a clear idea – we have a clear idea of how to act in any situation.'[109]

Think back to the Lionesses and the water bottle incident – and the lack of respect for the kit man. Many organizations have 'Respect' as one of their values. The incident showed how important it is to make sure values are clear and actionable. 'Respecting everyone around us' is a much more helpful articulation if you really want to make sure that it counts.

And the hidden power of the water bottle incident? The story it provides. The illustration it provides for everyone in terms of what's acceptable and what isn't; what's important and what's not.

Not backed up by clear behaviours

Sport is awash with examples of teams and organizations backing up their value statements with clarity on the behaviours that sit behind them. From Team Sky's Winning Behaviours app, aimed at getting the team aligned behind and cognizant of a set of positive everyday

---

[109] Simon Sinek, *Start With Why: How Great Leaders Inspire Everyone to Take Action*, Portfolio Penguin, 2011, p. 53.

actions,[110] through to the carefully agreed set of behaviours the GB Women's hockey squad set out in the Rio cycle, sport has long understood that in order to truly make your values count, you have to back them up with clear behaviours.

Beware though the two common mistakes that organizations make in this aspect: either shying away from trying to define behaviours at all (meaning that it's hard for your people to understand what your values actually mean) or drafting behavioural frameworks and requirements that are over-complicated and hard to follow.

Making Sure Values Drive Action

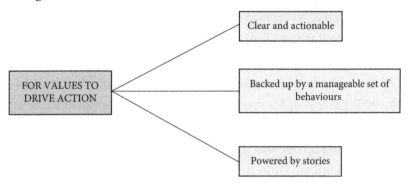

Asking for A and rewarding B

Too many organizations say the right things. Use the right words. Even display the right intention. And then let themselves down by how they praise, reward and promote their people. This is something coaches work incredibly hard at. Imagine my son's rugby team has set their values for the season and they are: 'We will constantly focus on what we can learn', 'We will look out for each other' and 'We will show respect to those around us at all times'. One Sunday they play a really

---

tough match; despite having the lead throughout the game, they just come up short at the end. In the huddle after the game, the coach will make sure that he reinforces and rewards the behaviour he has been asking for. He asks the players to reflect on and share what they have learnt from the game and congratulates the team for the brilliant way in which they looked out for one of their players who suffered a serious injury just after half-time. He is asking for A and rewarding A, which makes it much more likely that he will promote and elicit the behaviours he wants to see on a consistent and sustained basis.

Too many times organizations get this wrong. Having a value based around learning and yet not having any frameworks or systems in place that support and reward just that. Having a value based around respect and yet allowing all sorts of behaviour and approaches that reflect the opposite. Having a value based around collaboration and yet rewarding people for individual performance. How can you truly make your values count, if you are not backing them up in the way in which you reward your people?

So, how can you use and shape these lessons in your organizations?

Getting the Best Out of Your People – On a Sustained Basis

Recognize and play your role

Embrace your role in the culture of your organization. You have an important part to play in ensuring your values count. Play it. Doing so, playing your part in stitching the values into the fabric of your organization, will help ensure consistent performance that your people can sustain over the long term. And recognize that to make your values really count, you need to involve your people in the process; both in determining and agreeing the values and underlying behaviours and in regulating and policing what happens on the ground.

Be clear on what you mean

Make sure your values are clear, actionable and easy to understand. And backed up with specific and clear behaviours. Take this example from an organization I know well, a start-up in the world of intelligent appliances. They felt it was important to have a value around Doing the Right Thing so this is how they framed it:

We do the right thing

We are kind.

We look after each other. We are inclusive. We grow stronger through diversity.

We treat others how we would want to be treated.

We only say things about each other that we say to our faces.

We clean up after ourselves. We are humble enough to do the small things that need to be done.

We make sure we all have everything we need to be able to work safely and to work **better**.

And remember the power of stories as an effective way to demonstrate what your values mean and look like in practice.

Reinforce, reinforce, reinforce

Once you are clear on the behaviours that sit behind your values, be disciplined and relentless in reinforcing them. Catch the bad behaviour. Call it out. And, as importantly, make sure you pick up and put the spotlight on the right things. Weave the values and behaviours into your induction and onboarding process, your reward and recognition schemes, your promotion framework. And of course in those small coaching moments that we looked at in Chapter 11 (*see also* page 170) and that arise throughout the day and week.

From the field of play to the corridors of leadership

We met Leila in Chapter 9 when she took her charity through a process aimed at re-affirming a sense of belonging within the organization (*see also* page 143). We read that as part of this, the organization did a re-boot of their values. With each value, they made sure that they were clear and actionable. Leila particularly liked the way they framed the value on ever improving.

We are always improving

We are committed to making everything we do tomorrow **better** than it was today.

We never stop learning. Personal growth helps our organization grow.

We are curious; we are restless.

We are OK with failing as long as we fail fast, we learn from it and we do not blame others.

It's been a year now since the values have been in place. One thing Leila has learnt in particular has been the impact that she has on the success of these values. One day she had dropped into a workshop that a particular team were having; it was a good workshop, where some progress was made. As Leila went home that night, however, she reflected that the team had not been curious enough. They seemed too happy to accept statements and positions without really questioning them. And too keen to stay in their comfort zones and not push the boundaries. Leila realized she had missed an opportunity there to reinforce the values and make sure they really had impact. She had been listening to Ben Ryan's book, *Sevens Heaven*[111] (Ryan had coached

---

[111] Ben Ryan, *Sevens Heaven: The Beautiful Chaos of Fiji's Olympic Dream*, Weidenfeld & Nicolson, 2019.

the Fiji Sevens team to Olympic Gold at the Rio Olympics, the first Olympic Gold medal ever won by Fiji), and remembered his constant refrain: 'The standard you walk past is the standard you become'. She preferred this to the more conventional phrase with the word 'accept' and put a Post-it note on her monitor with this phrase so she could remind herself of it every day.

Leila realized through this how useful it was that they had set out clear behaviours under each value, as it really helped her to spot the gap. In the monthly internal newsletter, she asked if this story could be featured; demonstrating her mistake, her reflection and how she had since gone back to the team with her thoughts and comments and direction and support on how to truly live and keep each other accountable on the value of **We are always improving**.

In summary

- Your organization's values should guide everything that happens on the ground.
- Beware the pitfalls of under-playing or over-playing your hand as leader. Recognize and respect your role in making your organization's values count and the role of others.
- Make sure your values are clear, actionable and easy to understand.
- Back them up with clear behaviours.
- Remember the power of stories.
- Reinforce, reinforce, reinforce. The standard you walk past is the standard you become.

CHAPTER THIRTEEN

How to Navigate the Ownership Conundrum

'If you want to go fast, go alone. If you want to go far, go together.'

African proverb

There's a story that's famous in the world of coaching. It delivers a simple and powerful message through a world-leading coach getting something wrong.

In 2005, the All Blacks were coached by Graham Henry, one of the most experienced coaches in the world at that time. One day Henry was approached by the captain, Tana Umaga. Umaga asked Henry if they could have a coffee. Of course, Henry replied, thinking to himself, 'What's going on here?' After a bit of chat, Umaga got to the point: he asked Henry why he gave his team talk just before the players went out for a match. Henry thought about it and then replied by emphasizing that the purpose was to provide the team with a bit of motivation, a bit of direction, before the match. Umaga paused and asked his killer question: 'Ah, but are they for you or are they for us?'

The team talk had been part of Henry's ritual for 30 years. He liked to think he was pretty good at it but he realized Umaga was right. As he acknowledged at the time, the coaching staff spend the week before each game building the momentum of the group. As you do that, you transfer the responsibility from the coaches to the players. And then, an hour before the game, there is a person up the front telling them what to do.

Henry realized that it just didn't fit. He never gave another team talk. And he continued to try and develop, throughout the rest of his coaching career, the ability to empower his players in the right way – even going as far as to state that the aim of a coach should be to make themselves redundant. And the All Blacks? What happened when Henry's tenure came to an end in 2011 and Steve Hansen took over as head coach? They kept the approach in place. Hansen didn't conduct a single pre-match talk in his seven years in charge. In fact, he went one further: not giving half-time talks, but relying on the players to bring solutions to the table.[112] And their success rate under Hansen's tenure? An incredible 88.79 per cent winning record: 93 wins, four draws, 10 losses.

Umaga and Henry's story has always stayed with me. In particular because I have wanted to understand how it fits with leadership outside of sport. Is this a viable aim? Should this be what leaders work towards? Or is it not applicable or helpful outside of sport? After all, Lao Tzu, the sixth-century Chinese philosopher and author, is reputed to have said all those hundreds of years ago: 'A leader is best when people barely know he exists; when his work is done, his aim fulfilled, they will say – we did it ourselves.'

My conversation with coach Mel Marshall at the beginning of 2021 shed some useful light on this question. Mel's view was this: 'The ultimate aim of a great coach is to empower the people around them. I've always said, it's not about me – my results and how I am perceived – it has to be about them. You are in the wrong job if you are over-indulging in yourself and not making it about the athlete. Coaching is a selfless job and is all about how you illuminate the people you work with. Too often we prepare the road for the athlete. We must prepare the athlete for the road, empowering them to become independent learners and thinkers.'

---

[112] https://trainingground.guru/articles/why-the-all-blacks-ditched-pre-match-team-talks

Earlier in the book, we explored two of the three factors that Daniel Pink had identified in his book, *Drive* (*see also* page 62). The three factors that are in his view critical for motivation in the modern working world. We identified and discussed Purpose. And Mastery. And the third one? Autonomy. So what can we learn from sport to help solve what many leaders see as the ownership conundrum? After all, in the old days it was easy. Leaders were in charge. Leaders made the decisions. Leaders got stuff done. Now it's more of a minefield. We know the benefits of empowering others. We know that ownership needs to be distributed within our organizations. The world is too fast-paced and ever-changing for this not to be the case. And by not empowering everyone in your organization, you are missing a huge trick: that of utilizing and leveraging the knowhow, experience, expertise and perspective of everyone around you.

How can we get this right in a way that enables us as leaders to get the best out of our people, consistently, over the long term? And what can we learn from sport to help us?

How Do We Get This Wrong?

Ownership without responsibility

Phil Jackson is one of the most successful coaches of all time. As head coach of the Chicago Bulls and Los Angeles Lakers, Jackson won more championships than any coach in the history of his sport. Eleven times, he led his teams to the ultimate goal: the NBA championship. Six times with the Chicago Bulls and five times with the Los Angeles Lakers.

Jackson had a distinct style and approach, which he developed throughout his career. One of the first coaches to explore the benefits of mindfulness, he was constantly focused on trying to uncover the secrets of team chemistry and how to get the best out of his players. His philosophy and learnings are distilled down into his book written with Hugh Delehanty, *Eleven Rings*. Of the 'Jackson Eleven', his 11 principles of mindful leadership, number three focuses on this issue of ownership, autonomy and empowerment. Jackson says this: 'One thing I've learned as a coach is that you can't force your will on people. If you want them to act differently, you need to inspire them to change themselves. Most players are used to letting their coach think for them. When they run into a problem on the court, they look nervously over at the sidelines, expecting coach to come up with an answer. Many coaches will gladly accommodate them. But not me. I've always been interested in getting players to think for themselves so that they can make difficult decisions in the heat of the battle.'[113]

And it seemed to work pretty well for him.

Part of this is about taking responsibility. And this time we will turn to some Norwegian athletes to show us the way. One of the stories that Owen Slot, in his book *The Talent Lab*, explores is that of Norway's reaction to their uncharacteristic failure in the 2006 Winter Olympics in Turin. Accustomed to finishing top of the cross-country medal table, they had come in seventh. Their response was to put together a crack team of physiologists, psychologists, historians, former athletes and coaches to try and get to the bottom of what had changed. The information and data that they discovered was distilled down into the ultimate success manual, a book called *Den Norske Langrennsboka* (*The Norwegian Book of Cross-Country Skiing*).[114] And the result of all this work? A significant turnaround in the team's fortunes; by 2015, they had won nine of the 12 Golds in the cross-country events of the world championships in Falun.

You can appreciate that the contents of the manual were now pretty valuable intellectual property. In the spirit of cross-nation sharing and collaboration, the Norwegian experts entertained a small group

---

[113] Phil Jackson and Hugh Delehanty, *Eleven Rings*, Virgin Books, 2015, p. 13.
[114] Sandbakk, Øyvind Tønnessen, Espen, *Den Norske Langrennsboka*, Aschehoug, 2012.

of British Olympic coaches who had come to discover some of the secrets of their performance in this discipline. And one of the things they learnt was this: the nature of the cross-country training regime requires a lot of training and a lot of long distances. This means that 80 per cent of the work has to be done solo or away from the eyes of the coaches. Meaning that the cross-country coaches have to let their athletes go and just trust them. In the Norwegian system now every young athlete is required to record a training diary. Not only does this mean a significant database and feedback system for the national federation, it also means that the young athletes are encouraged to understand and interpret their own training data. As Slot says, because they effectively self-train, they are encouraged, as far as possible, to self-coach. And he goes on to say that there is evidence that one discriminatory factor between those who are and who are not successful in their ability to do this is the extent to which they take ownership.[115]

And this, I think, goes to the heart of the issue. We know that allowing a level of ownership in the workplace can drive motivation and better outcomes. With this ownership though must come a willingness and desire to take the consequences. Ownership is both a privilege and responsibility. For the budding Norwegian skiers coming through the ranks, it's not just those who are not prepared to take ownership of their training that you want to worry about. It's also those who are happy to be given ownership, and control, and yet are not prepared to take responsibility for the outcomes. What you really want is those who relish the ownership *and* also relish the responsibility. And are prepared to be accountable for the outcomes, rather than passing the buck back onto the coaching staff.

---

[115] Owen Slot, *The Talent Lab: The Secrets of Creating and Sustaining Success*, Ebury Press, 2017, pp. 187–9.

Discounting the power of 'us'

There are some common and consistent pushbacks on distributing ownership. That it is time-consuming. That you are never going to get a consensus. That too many cooks spoil the broth. When I hear these (and I do hear them quite a lot), I always come back to this mantra: short-term pain for long-term gain.

It might be a bit messier to start with. Progress might be a bit slower. But there's no point getting to your destination if no one has come with you. Think back to Graham Henry and the struggle he must have had not just to change the habit of a lifetime, but also to resist stepping in and taking over again (*see also* page 187). The results at first might not have been what he wanted to see. There will undoubtedly have been times when Henry felt a few words from him might have made all the difference but he let the players own the situation, let them have control, let them feel the responsibility, and the ultimate results meant that he never did a team talk again.

You will get more out of your people, on a long-term basis, if they own the outcomes which they and their teams are working towards. *And* where they have seen and understood the real magic: that when their team does well, this benefits them as individuals. Phil Jackson is more qualified than most to make this point. One of his most significant challenges when coaching the Chicago Bulls was to help Michael Jordan understand that he needed his team, that it couldn't just be a one-man show. And, more than, this, that the focus on team and developing the whole would give Jordan a greater chance of achieving his own personal goals.

Lack of capability

In order for this transfer of ownership to happen successfully, however, your people have to be proficient. They need to have the required skillsets. You need to have invested in building the right organizational capability. We have explored already Netflix's distinct approach and culture (*see also* page 140). In her book, *Powerful: Building a Culture of Freedom and Responsibility*, Patty McCord, co-creator of the famous Netflix culture deck and chief talent officer there from 1998–2012, emphasized the importance of anchoring freedom and responsibility with capability. She shares her approach to helping teams address challenges ahead of them.

The starting point is to imagine six months from now, you have the most amazing team you have ever assembled. The next step is to write down what the team will be accomplishing in six months' time that it's not accomplishing now. Next (and this is where the real magic starts), think about how things are being done differently from the way they are currently done. Are people working more cross-functionally? Doing more collaborative problem-solving? Have they developed greater project management skillsets? And the next step? You will have guessed it. McCord asks: in order for those different things to be happening, what would people need to know how to do? What kind of skills and experiences would it take for the team to operate in the way you're describing and accomplish the things you'll need to do in that future?[116] And this is the problem that many organizations make: they devolve ownership, without making sure their people have the skills to use it properly. Without making sure the right systems and processes are in place to facilitate it.

You have to work hard at it – it doesn't just happen. And to reinforce this, we will turn as our final sports story to one of the most important initiatives that the GB Women's Hockey coaching team put into place for the squad in the build-up to the Rio Olympic Games:

[116] Patty McCord, *Powerful: Building a Culture of Freedom and Responsibility*, Silicon Guild, 2018, pp. 76–7.

'Thinking Thursdays'. Wednesday night would find the players desperately checking their emails. Not to get news from friends and family, or catch up with personal admin, but to pick up *that* email; the email containing the instructions for the next day's tournament. Each week, different formats, different teams and different rules were set. The players had complete ownership, from the moment the email dropped, for organizing their teams and planning their approach. The goal was simple: to win the next day's tournament. Players became as motivated to lead the Thinking Thursday wins table as they were to win Olympic Gold.

There was a further twist: during the tournament each Thursday, the coaching staff would throw in all sorts of things to throw the players off-balance, from changes of rules through to new outcomes. Throwing in an element of chaos. Testing recall. And testing and building the ability of the players to think on their feet. And adapt. Fast.

The purpose behind this initiative? To build the players' ability to own the outcome. To take responsibility for it. And to give them the toolkit to do so.

So how can we get this right from a leadership point of view in order to drive consistent performance from our people over the long term?

Getting the Best Out of Your People – On a Sustained Basis

Your role

So much of what we have uncovered in this book points to a different type of leadership than has historically been the norm. Rather than a leader who has all the answers, a leader who is comfortable admitting that they don't. Rather than a leader who is all-powerful, a leader who goes about their business more quietly, with more of focus on listening, and with a mindset centred on continuous improvement. A leader who chooses their words carefully. Who focuses on developing their people for the long term and ensuring the right conditions are in place to allow this to happen.

'Command and control' have been left behind to be replaced by 'direction and clarity'. Leaders provide the direction. They provide clarity on what's important. And then they let others get on with the job. Chicago Bulls coach Phil Jackson understood this: 'After years of experimenting, I discovered that the more I tried to exert power directly, the less powerful I became. I learned to dial back my ego and distribute power as widely as possible without surrendering final authority. Paradoxically, this approach strengthened my effectiveness because it freed me to focus on my job as keeper of the team's vision.'[117] And from Jackson to another exceptional leader: Jack Ma, co-founder and former executive chairman of the Alibaba Group, the phenomenally successful technology conglomerate. At a young leaders' session in Davos in 2018, he told the delegates that his job as leader was to set the vision, hire really good people and then ensure the conditions which allow them to work together towards that vision.[118]

In today's fast-paced and ever-changing world, you can't hold all the power at the top. It's not going to facilitate long-term success. Not only must you involve others, you have to also give them a clear sense of ownership. Provide the direction. Give them the clarity they need. And then give them the ownership that ensures that the outcomes belong to them. As individuals, as teams and as the whole organization.

---

[117] Phil Jackson and Hugh Delehanty, *Eleven Rings*, Virgin Books, 2015, p. 12.
[118] https://www.youtube.com/watch?v=4zzVjonyHcQ

Equip your people with the right skills

In order to make this work, you need to build the right capability within the organization. Take the time to look into the future. Try and understand what abilities and skillsets the organization will need to have this thread of ownership running through everything so that teams and individuals really can own their projects, tasks and outcomes, rather than having to have someone step in at the last minute and take over. Build the ability to make decisions, work collaboratively, problem solve, think strategically, project manage … And whatever else is needed for successful outcomes in your organization over the long term.

Reinforce

Are you doing all you can to truly embed and reinforce a culture of ownership? What kind of language are you using? Do you refer to 'my organization', 'my outcomes' and 'my vision' or 'our organization', 'our outcomes' and 'our vision'? Remember the power of the language that we use.

Does your organization facilitate and promote ownership from the first day someone joins? From the bottom all the way through to the top? Are your systems and processes aligned behind this? It's no good expecting your people, when they reach a certain level in the business, to take ownership of outcomes if they haven't been trained in that way from the start. Does your reward and recognition framework support and encourage this? Is your training reinforced on a regular basis? Are you really doing all you can? Too many leaders hold their hands up and say: 'I've tried to devolve ownership to my people but it always goes wrong. They just aren't capable.' If that's the case, whose fault is it? You have to have the right scaffolding in place.

From the field of play to the corridors of leadership

Yael has just taken a big decision: she has accepted the role of CEO at a large corporate within her sector. She thought very carefully about this decision for one main reason: the outgoing CEO had run the company in a very directive way, very much following the command and control style of leadership. As a result, the company had lost good people and needed a re-boot. Yael was worried that her style was going to be such a contrast however that the people within the business would struggle with the change.

She reached out to her mentor before she made her decision. Her mentor ran a large organization in another sector and led much more in the way that Yael did and believed in. Her mentor's advice was that this was a good opportunity for Yael and that she should take it. And that she should stay true to her style of leadership. But he warned her that she would need to put the work in first. The organization wouldn't be able, overnight, to become one where a true sense of ownership was the norm. There would be nothing worse than coming in and trying to drive a culture of ownership, without having built the capability within the organization first; this would no doubt lead to Yael (and other senior leaders) seeing the need to step into things at the last minute, which would be of no long-term benefit to anyone or the organization itself.

Yael's mentor advised that one of her first tasks would be to ascertain the level of ownership in the business already, then examine how people dealt with the level of ownership they had. And then reflect on how much things needed to change. She should then, along with her senior leadership team, go through an exercise where they determined what the gaps were and put together a plan focused on building the relevant skillsets and attributes. Finally, her mentor reminded Yael that this shouldn't be a one-hit wonder; the drive to foster a feeling of ownership throughout the organization needed to be backed up by continuous learning; systems and processes that supported it and recruitment, reward and recognition frameworks that endorsed it.

In summary

- The old model of leader as the All-Mighty is not fit for purpose any more.
- Your people need direction and clarity, not command and control.
- Devolving ownership breeds motivation and engagement and better outcomes over time.
- It also gives your organization an improved chance of sustained success over the long term, ensuring you utilize and leverage the knowhow, experience, expertise and perspective of everyone in your organization.
- But it doesn't just happen. You have to equip the people in your organization with the right skillsets, provide the opportunities and training to build this.
- You have to help them understand that with ownership comes responsibility. Reinforce this at all times.
- And you need to put the scaffolding in place to support this: use the right language and make sure you have the right systems and processes in place.
- Ownership can't be an add-on or an after-thought. It has to be part of your organization's DNA.

Final Thoughts: It Really
Is a Marathon, Not a Sprint

I live in York, in the north of England. It's roughly a two-hour train journey from London. About a year into the COVID-19 pandemic, when travelling for work was allowed, I found myself sitting in a carriage on the train down to London with just two women: one older, one younger. Despite the reading I was meant to be doing my attention was soon captured by their conversation, especially when I heard the younger one saying, 'This is just not sustainable, either for me or my staff.' To which the older woman replied by saying something along the lines of 'You are right. It's like we've all had to be sprinting over the last few months. But we can't carry on like this for ever. It's been an enforced sprint within what is ultimately a marathon. You will need to reset the approach and pace if you want to be able to sustain performance.'

Leadership matters. And as leaders, you have the power within your hands to have a significant impact through your roles. Both as an individual, and via your organization. The more you can sustain your, and your organization's performance, and the more you can consistently get the best out of yourself and your people, the greater that impact is going to be over the long term.

Since overhearing this conversation and then setting out to write this book, I have had conversations with many leaders to test my beliefs about what was important to sustained performance and what needed to be included. My conversations with those right at the coalface reinforced the need to build the stamina muscle not just for themselves, but also for those they lead. And that while I was clear that sport really could show us the way, these lessons had not been either glimpsed, or truly understood, by those around me. And so I hope that this book provides you with the lessons and the tools for your own long-term leadership journey; that ensures you can stay the distance and that you enjoy every single step along the way.

Reading List

In writing *Staying the Distance*, my thinking has been informed by a variety of books, as follows. I would like to thank all the authors for educating and inspiring me.

Atomic Habits by James Clear (Random House Business, 2018)

Becoming a True Athlete: A Practical Philosophy for Flourishing Through Sport by Laurence Cassøe Halstead (Sequoia Books, 2021)

Belonging: The Ancient Code of Togetherness by Owen Eastwood (Quercus Editions Ltd, 2021)

Black Box Thinking: The Surprising Truth About Success by Matthew Syed (John Murray (Publishers), 2015)

Bounce: Mozart, Federer, Picasso, Beckham, and the Science of Success by Matthew Syed (HarperCollins, 2010)

Dare to Lead: Brave Work. Tough Conversations. Whole Hearts by Brené Brown (Vermilion, 2018)

Drive: The Surprising Truth About What Motivates Us by Daniel Pink (Canongate Books, 2011)

Drop the Pink Elephant: 15 Ways to Say What You Mean...and Mean What You Say by Bill McFarlan (Capstone Publishing Ltd, 2004)

Eleven Rings by Phil Jackson and Hugh Delehanty (Virgin Books, 2015)

Fear Less: How to Win at Life Without Losing Yourself by Dr Pippa Grange (Vermilion, 2020)

Fortitude: Unlocking the Secrets of Inner Strength by Bruce Daisley (Cornerstone Press, 2022)

How to Win: Rugby and Leadership from Twickenham to Tokyo by Sir Clive Woodward (Hodder & Stoughton, 2019)

Leaders Eat Last: Why Some Teams Pull Together and Others Don't by Simon Sinek (Penguin, 2017)

Legacy: What the All Blacks Can Teach Us About the Business of Life by James Kerr (Constable & Robinson Ltd, 2013)

Micro-Resilience: Minor Shifts for Major Boosts in Focus, Drive and Energy by Bonnie St John and Allen Haines (Piatkus, 2017)

Mindset: Changing the Way You Think to Fulfil Your Potential by Dr Carol Dweck (Robinson, 2012)

Range: How Generalists Triumph in a Specialized World by David Epstein (Macmillan, 2019)

Relentless: Secrets of the Sporting Elite by Alistair Brownlee (Harper Collins Publishers, 2021)

Relentless: From Good to Great to Unstoppable by Tim S. Grover with Shari Lesser Wenk (Scribner, 2014)

Rest: Why You Get More Done When You Work Less by Alex Soojung-Kim Pang (Penguin Life, 2018)

Sevens Heaven: The Beautiful Chaos of Fiji's Olympic Dream by Ben Ryan (Weidenfeld & Nicolson, 2019)

Start With Why: How Great Leaders Inspire Everyone to Take Action by Simon Sinek (Portfolio Penguin, 2009)

Switch: How to Change Things When Change is Hard by Chip and Dan Heath (Random House Business Books, 2011)

The Captain Class: The Hidden Force Behind the World's Greatest Teams by Sam Walker (Ebury Press, 2017)

The Culture Code: The Secrets of Highly Successful Groups by Daniel Coyle (Bantam Books, 2018)

The Expectation Effect: How Your Mindset Can Transform Your Life by David Robson (Canongate Books, 2022)

The Fearless Organization: Creating Psychological Safety in the Workplace for Learning, Innovation and Growth by Amy Edmondson (John Wiley & Sons, Inc., 2019)

The Infinite Game by Simon Sinek (Penguin Business Books, 2019)

The Long Win: The Search for a Better Way to Succeed by Cath Bishop (Practical Inspiration Publishing, 2020)

The Mindset of Success: From Good Management to Great Leadership by Jo Owen (Kogan Page Limited, 2015)

The Optimism Bias: Why We're Wired to Look on the Bright Side by Tali Sharot (Robinson, 2012)

The Pressure Principle: Handle Stress, Harness Energy, and Perform When It Counts by Sir Dave Alred (Penguin Life, 2016)

The Promises of Giants: How YOU Can Fill the Leadership Void by John Amaechi OBE (Nicholas Brealey Publishing, 2021)

The Score Takes Care of Itself: My Philosophy of Leadership by Bill Walsh with Steve Jamison and Craig Walsh (The Penguin Group, 2010)

The Talent Lab: The Secrets of Creating and Sustaining Success by Owen Slot (Ebury Press, 2017)

Think Again: The Power of Knowing What You Don't Know by Adam Grant (WH Allen, 2021)

Winners: And How They Succeed by Alistair Campbell (Hutchinson, 2015)

Winning Not Fighting: Why You Need to Rethink Success and How You Achieve it with the Ancient Art of Wing Tsun by John Vincent and Sifu Julian Hitch (Penguin Business, 2019)

Acknowledgements

My first thank you must go to all the athletes and coaches whose stories and insight have provided the platform for this book.

Thank you also to all the authors who have inspired my thinking and shown me the way (*see* Reading List for details).

Thank you to all those who have given me the privilege of letting me work with and alongside you over the last few years in particular; each and every one of you has shaped my thinking and increased my learning. These include: Nigel Clarke; Emily Clarke; Stuart Bell; Phil Hardy; Nicola Woolner; Kingsley Johnson; Alex Mayfield; Paul Kelly; Chris Recchia; Emma Atkins; Marc Tobias; Gareth Brahams; Tara Dillon; Mark Gannon; Will Lambe; Simone Pennie; Samantha Lake Coghlan; Alisa Gray; Dan Kayne; Tony Massarella; Max Gower; Zoe Robinson; Deborah Boylan; Kirsty Medway; Tim Hollingsworth.

Thank you to my early readers, who did so much to help hone and sharpen the manuscript: Alan Dunsmore; Cath Bishop; Sara Karlen Lacombe; Nick Fuller; Andy Falconer.

Thank you to Alison Jones, whose role as my book coach was invaluable.

Thank you to my husband, Gary Baker, whose careful, patient and informed feedback improved the book exponentially, and who has provided immense support along the way.

Thank you to my three sons, Barney, Joseph and Toby, who teach me something new each and every day.

Thank you to the many friends who have given me huge amounts of encouragement as I have set about this task, including in particular Rachel Dunsmore, Cherry Fricker, Jenny Black, Kate Newbold, Charlotte Cornwallis and Kate Harpin.

Thank you to my twin sister, Nicola, who has always shown complete faith and belief in my endeavours. Anyone who has a twin will know how special that bond is.

And finally, thank you to two women without whose support on the domestic front over the years I would not have had the time and space to do what I do: Polly Reynolds and Samantha Hunter.

Index

Note: page numbers in **bold** refer to diagrams.

Landin, Lasse 160–1, 163–4
Landy, John 119
language use 51–2, 54, 150–1
   see also inner dialogue
Lao Tzu 188
Lavallee, David 17–18, 66
learning cultures 167–8, 171–4
Lee, Matty 104
letting go 95–6
limits/limitations 41, 94
listening skills 80–1, 153–4, 195
Liverpool FC 135
Loehr, James 91–2, 96–7
Lombardi, Vince 26
London 2012 Olympics 17, 85, 103, 145
London Pulse 131, 133–4, 140
long-termism 159–74
Lord's 31–2
Los Angeles Lakers 117–18, 189

Ma, Jack 195
Macleod, Hannah 32
mantras 113, 134
Marshall, Mel 11, 21, 27–8, 171, 188
Marylebone Cricket Club (MCC) 31
mastery 12, 34, 59–62, 68, **68**, 71, 169, 189
McCord, Patty 193
McFarlan, Bill 150
McKinsey & Company 90, 95, 133, 139–40, 161
mental models 120
messages 151–3, 156, 170–1
Metropolitan Police 134
micro breaks 91–2, 96–7
Microsoft 89, 126, 168, 176
Microsoft Model Coach Care 173
mindfulness 189–90
mindsets 48–55, 120, 195
   challenge 48–55, **53**
   fixed 20, 21, 23
   growth 20–4, 26–7, 40, 76–7, 108, 126–7, 130,
      155, 168, 172
   threat 48–55, **53**
Moore, Michelle 39
Morgan, Alex 73
Morley, David 171–2
motivation 74–7, 163, 189
   away-from 39
   fear-based 34–5
   and money 58–9
   and ownership 191
   and setbacks 77
   and success 75
   sustained 57–71
   towards 39

Nadal, Rafael 31, 67, 86
Nadella, Satya 89, 126, 168, 176, 179

National Basketball Association (NBA) 117–18,
   139, 189
National Collegiate Athletic Association (NCAA)
   103
Navratilova, Martina 57
negativity 33–5, 37, 39
netball 131–4, 140, 175–6
Netflix 140, 193
Neville, Phil 175
Neville, Tracey 175–6
New York Times 137
no, learning to say 89, 94
non-verbal communication 148–9, 151–3, 155
norms, group 136–7
Norway 190–1

O Shaped Lawyer 161
opportunity cost 87
organizational culture 12, 167–8, 171–4, 176–80,
   183, 193, 196
organizational values 172, 175–86
Östersund FK 159–61, 163, 169–70
outcomes 12, 59–62, 120–1
Owen, Michael 135
ownership 187–98

Pakhalina, Yulia 103
panic 43–4
Paralympians 61
partners 70–1
pauses 95
Peaty, Adam 11, 21, 27–8, 171
Pentland, Alex 'Sandy' 153–4
people pleasers 95
perfectionism 36–7, 40–1
performance 15, 101–2, 125, 145, 191
   and confidence 17–20, 25
   and discipline 75, 77–82
   and emotions 44–55
   and fear 32, 33–5, 37–40
   and focus 11, 13
   over-estimation of your 164–5
   and range 162, 169
   sustainable 11, 13–14, 18–20, 33–5, 37–40,
      47–55, 78–82, 88–9, 93–8, 145
   and time management skills 86–9,
      93–8
   and trust 109
   and wellbeing 89–90, **90**
periodization, effort 92–3
perspective 65–6, 69, 70
Peters, Steve 44, 45
Pink, Daniel 62–5, 189
'pink elephants' 150
positivity 32, 34–5, 37, 39, 55
Potter, Graham 159–60
pre-frontal cortex 46, 48